Circling Home

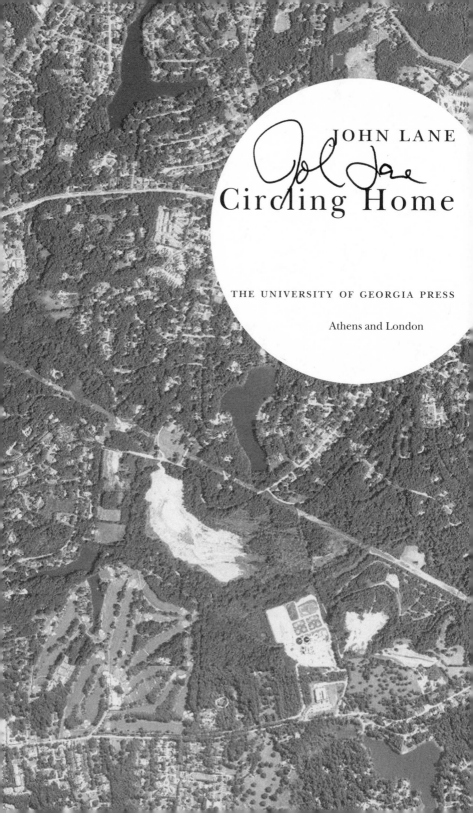

JOHN LANE

Circling Home

THE UNIVERSITY OF GEORGIA PRESS

Athens and London

Published by the University of Georgia Press
Athens, Georgia 30602
wwww.ugapress.org
© 2007 by John Lane
All rights reserved
Designed by David Drummond & Kathi Morgan
Set in ITC New Baskerville by BookComp
Printed and bound by Thomson-Shore
The paper in this book meets the guidelines for
permanence and durability of the Committee on
Production Guidelines for Book Longevity of the
Council on Library Resources.
Printed in the United States of America
11   10   09   08   C   5   4   3   2
Library of Congress Cataloging-in-Publication Data
Lane, John, 1954–
Circling home / John Lane.
        p. cm.
"A Wormsloe Foundation nature book."
ISBN-13: 978-0-8203-3040-2 (hardcover : alk. paper)
ISBN-10: 0-8203-3040-X (hardcover : alk. paper)
1. Lane, John, 1954– —Homes and haunts—South
Carolina—Spartanburg.   2. Spartanburg (S.C.)—
Biography.   3. Spartanburg (S.C.)—Description and
travel.   4. Natural history—South Carolina—
Spartanburg.   5. Naturalists—United States—Biography.
6. Outdoor life—United States.   I. Wormsloe Foundation.
II. Title.
F279.S7L36 2007
975.7'29—dc22   2007016765
British Library Cataloging-in-Publication Data available
Title page image provided by GlobeXplorer.com

FOR FRANKLIN BURROUGHS

I think of no natural feature which is a greater ornament and treasure to this town than the river. It is one of the things which determine whether a man will live here or in another place, and it is one of the first objects which we show to a stranger. . . . They who laid out the town should have made the river available as a common possession forever.

HENRY DAVID THOREAU, *Wild Fruits*

Contents

The Circle

within one mile of our house

Pierce Acr

Lake Forest
Drive

Fred's Cache

Starline
Drive

The Clear-cut

Lawson's Fork
Creek

The Country Club

The Sewer
Treatment Plant

Country Club Road

Oak Creek
Plantation

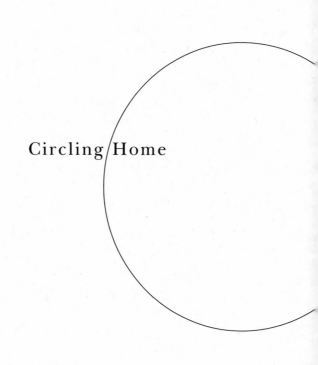

Circling Home

I live my life in growing orbits,
Which move out over the things of the world.
RAINER MARIA RILKE, *The Book of Hours*,
translated by Robert Bly

Drawing the Circle

When Betsy and I moved into this house on Lawson's Fork Creek in 2003 I tried the old rituals that had always worked to settle me when I lived alone: I placed my favorite books on a bookshelf close at hand—collected hardback editions of poetry, a few volumes of nature essays, and several field guides to birds and snakes. On the freshly painted wall of the study I hung my "Inward Society: Surrealism and Recent American Poetry" festival poster (circa 1982). It features René Magritte's painting *The Month of Grape-Gathering*, with a crowd of men in black bowlers looking through an open window into a blue room. I've always loved those men in suits and see them as a surreal vision of what could have become of me had my life turned out differently.

In the corner I propped the six-foot hand-carved canoe paddle I'd brought back from floating a river in the rain forests of Suriname. It's to remind me of all the travels it took to bring me to settle.

1

I also hauled boxes of fossils out of storage in the basement and placed on top of the bookshelf part of the lower jawbone of a Pleistocene mastodon that I'd found on the beach at Edisto Island along South Carolina's coast while I was still in college in the seventies.

Finally, as always, next to the fragment of the mastodon jawbone I made a vertical stack of the nine books of poetry and prose I'd published in the last fifteen years as a writer, as if to say—in some way I didn't fully understand—"this pile of books equals this fossil."

The paint color I chose for the study was "apple cider," but most would call it orange, not a very manly color for what traditionally has been a very "manly" room. I like the color though.

As the old joke goes, sometimes I sit in this study and think, and sometimes I just sit. Betsy ceded this room to me for this purpose, to give me a spot to meditate, write, reflect. It's worked so far. There are more questions than answers hanging here since we moved in.

How do we decide where to dream a life into existence? On what scrap of this vast planet should we hammer in our stakes and say "home"? How do we live there with our neighbors? What level of commitment to landscape is acceptable? What lack of awareness is unacceptable? These are some of the questions I began this book with. I decided to answer them as best I could through what my geologist-archaeologist friend Terry Ferguson calls "ground-truthing."

Ground-truthing is verification by direct evidence obtained when you visit a place after having seen it in the abstract on a map or an aerial photograph. It is the truth you can find by interacting with the real world and examining a place and recording the data about it. What follows is the story of my own field experience in search of direct evidence. It's also turned out to be a record of what could be called my own theory and practice of settlement.

For the next six months, our first in our new house, I sat daily with my back to the big south-facing windows, ready to write. The work came in fits and starts. I was able to finish up a few new poems and wrote a sloppy draft of an essay about paddling a wild river, but when I wrote letters and answered e-mails I talked instead about what I wanted to write, the book perking within me already, about the floodplain and the creek, called Lawson's Fork, out beyond the big windows, our new home ground, and how love and marriage had brought me here to settle on it.

I know it might seem at first like there's nothing strange or noteworthy about a marriage or building a house in the woods, but I also know that it was noteworthy to me because these things happened to me quite late in life, and because I've always had such a deep unexplored relationship with this place where I grew up. I'm an apple, as they say, that didn't fall far from the tree, but I've spent so little time climbing around in the branches of that very tree.

The neighborhood we built in was near what my mother called "Pill Hill." When I was a kid we cruised through here on lazy Sunday afternoons and looked at the big houses set back from the road on acre lots where, my mother explained from our rattle-trap, cantaloupe-colored DeSoto's front seat, "the rich people lived."

Most would say I got lucky after a childhood here in Spartanburg with the diminished expectations that usually come with southern poverty. I finished high school and even got a college degree. I didn't land in a dead-end job in a textile plant barely hanging on against foreign competition or get lucky in another way and end up working for the Germans on the line at BMW. I went to college, traveled, taught and wrote poetry, worked for a raft company in the mountains, and then finally I ended up back here in Spartanburg teaching at the school I'd attended as an undergraduate. In 1988 I finally landed like a maple seed. I began working as an English professor and writer in a Carolina piedmont landscape reserved for two hundred years mostly for commerce, not reflection.

Now nearly twenty years later, approaching fifty, I have a good wife, a ready-made family, a new architect-designed house on the east side of town, a tenured career as a college professor, and all the daily responsibilities that go along with it all. I'm one of those people in a big house with a big mortgage to prove it.

The January after we moved in I got lucky again. I was given an unexpected month off from teaching responsibilities, and I decided to seize the freedom and begin to get to know this place we'd settled in. Maps can give perspective, so I purchased a topographic map over the Internet, and when it arrived I unrolled it back in my study. I placed four gray river rocks on the corners to hold the map open on the black linoleum surface of my new desk and tried to orient myself within its formal borders.

This map, called a quadrangle, is a two-foot-square green, red, and white expanse that symbolizes the change that human settlement like ours has created on a landscape. It hasn't been updated in thirty years, so our street but not our house shows up on its printed surface. The map is green where there was forest cover, and blue lines stand in for waterways and brown continuous squiggles for contour lines (some as tightly bunched as a fingerprint where the land is steep), but there are also white expanses for clearings and black lines for roads and boundaries. Small black dots represent houses and bold black blocks stand in for schools, mills, and factories.

It's the most detailed map of our new home ground I could find. The map is called a 7.5-minute series, a quarter of a degree of the earth's surface. This particular one is a single square out of several hundred or so that cover the cartographic expanse of this landscape known as South Carolina.

Our quadrangle is located in the northwest of the state, and it covers an area about seven miles by ten miles, a perfect rectangle of territory. That's not much land—seventy square miles—

in a state with thirty-one thousand total. The United States Geological Service calls this particular quad "the Pacolet Quadrangle". The name comes from the river town of Pacolet in the quad's northern quarter.

The map describes a section of South Carolina piedmont landscape no one would go as far as to call dramatic. Around here, it's not the coast, and it's not the mountains. It's somewhere in between. Once, 150 million years ago, we had charismatic mountains like those in Peru, but erosion had its way with them. The natural process of water working down mountains put over a hundred miles of coastal plain and Piedmont between the oceanfront property and us.

Half the piedmont is abandoned farmland, and many of its cities are sprawling outward to envelop what's left of the forests. There are no national parks celebrating the piedmont landscape, no large tracts of hill country set aside and preserved. People think of this landscape mostly as working class earning its way. "The piedmont's either plowed, paved, or in succession," Michael Godfrey says famously in his *Naturalist's Guide to the Piedmont.*

Through the center of the topo, in the territory behind our house, runs the course of the very real Lawson's Fork Creek, a mostly overlooked waterway we've learned over time to love with a depth that friends have pointed out to us doesn't seem to match the piedmont creek's character. There are bigger waterways in the county, such as the Tyger, Pacolet, or Enoree Rivers, but for complex reasons our love of this creek showed up even before we built here on the edge of its floodplain. Out beyond my study windows flows its watery landscape, both real and imagined. It's what Betsy and I seized on together soon after we fell in love.

In some ways our relationship with it began with a mutual dream. We didn't know each other before a group began gathering at a local coffee shop downtown in the midnineties. I began to talk over coffee with two local journalists, Betsy and Gary

Henderson, about literary community in Spartanburg—or the lack of it. We soon proposed publishing an anthology of personal essays describing what it was like to live here. All three of us would write essays for it, and Betsy and I would edit it. Out of that coffee klatch the Hub City Writers Project was founded in 1996. We wanted to give Spartanburg a literary identity in a time of what looked to us like an imaginative depression, so we named the organization after the Federal Writers Project of the 1930s in hopes that it would put writers to work for our community. We sketched out the first book project on a napkin, and it all evolved from there into what is now a community-based nonprofit with thirty books behind it, a yearly budget of over three hundred thousand dollars, and its own building.

At the time Betsy and I didn't know we'd find love in our effort to build a literary community. We seemed an odd couple to some. Betsy is from a family of Spartanburg social and cultural insiders. I literally grew up on the other side of the tracks. My father died when I was five and my mother never remarried. She raised my sister and me in a series of cheap rental houses, paying the bills with Social Security checks and my dead father's tiny V.A. pension.

But we did fall in love, and Betsy is now director of Hub City, our mutual dream. In 2000, four years after that beginning, we published a book celebrating this creek by David Taylor and Gary Henderson, *The Lawson's Fork: Headwaters to Confluence*, organized a four-day festival to launch its publication, and financed a thirty-minute video—all to introduce the community to what Betsy calls "Spartanburg's historic watery main street." Naturalist Robert Michael Pyle came to town and caught butterflies along the creek, activist and writer Janisse Ray explored it for a week as a Hub City writer-in-residence, and writer Barry Lopez walked the trails and helped us see our local creek in a new light.

When Lopez was in town someone asked him how to address

an impaired creek like Lawson's Fork, and he said, "It's not the creek that's impaired, it's our relationship with it." By the time the festival was over we'd set out to pay attention to this spoiled, ragged waterway shaded by leaning river birch and box elder. We'd even embraced its ugly side, the abandoned tires and garbage washed down from the urban center of Spartanburg. We made a vow that our relationship to it would be different from what we'd seen in the past.

What's beautiful about the creek is still hard to articulate even after books and videos and testimonials by some of the country's leading nature writers, but we found it impossible to abandon once we'd fallen for it. By building a house here we took a deeper vow—to stay bound to its course, its moods, for richer or for poorer, in sickness and in health.

Where I grew up in Spartanburg, I was mostly unaware of the creek's presence. My childhood was spent on the crass, commercial west side of town in another creek's watershed, far off the map I now pore over in my study. Even in college when I fell in love with boats and the sparkling white water of the mountains to the west, Lawson's Fork, this mild, dirty piedmont stream with a few shoals, escaped my search for falling water and the excitement it always brings.

I admire almost any person who shows up with a cause or any natural landscape that displays one by its existence. I tend to gravitate toward the vulnerable, the outsider, the underdog, and in our community there were few to look out for this waterway, so we took it on. Now, living next to Lawson's Fork, I respect it like a working-class neighbor, at moments even love it like a family member. For 175 years it's carried on with the hard labor of disappearing our garbage and sewage. It's hauled the burden of our neglect, abandonment, and abuse. Once I met this creek what was I to do but love it?

Betsy is tall and slim and blond. She throws herself into whatever she does—writing and editing, publishing, child-raising, marriage. She works best when there are heavy demands and expectations. She is an idealist who grew up believing in the power of words and actions.

She really began with more of a claim to the creek than I had. She grew up swimming in Lawson's Fork's watershed, in a suburban lake up on a short tributary a little more than a mile from where we built. She's the one who has really come home, now living not far from where her mother and father live.

As our first months passed in the new house, I looked over the square expanse of the quadrangle, and I finally figured out that I wanted more focus than it offered, so one day on a whim I walked back to the kitchen and opened the cabinets and pulled out an old chipped white saucer and carried it through the dining and living rooms to my study. I measured the saucer against the scale on the topo map still held flat by the river rocks and noticed that if I placed the plate's center over the spot where our house would be when the map was finally updated, the diameter would be the equivalent of two miles, every radius a mile out from the center in all directions. I picked up a Sharpie from the desk and etched a black line around the perimeter of the plate, defining what I hoped would soon become familiar ground.

What was amazing was the way enclosing the landscape in a tight circle brought into dramatic relief how much was contained within so small an area. I studied the map and inventoried what I already knew from local lore was contained in the circle: a stretch of gneiss shoals with waterfalls protected by a land trust, a site where a friend had found an eight-thousand-year-old cache of Archaic period Native American artifacts, the site of a vanished ironworks from the eighteenth century, a Revolutionary War site and the graves of a dozen British soldiers killed there in August of 1780, the remnants of two cotton plantations settled just after the Revolution, a historic mill village founded in 1835, the one-hundred-year-old Country Club of

Spartanburg, a sewer treatment plant over seventy years old, an old-folks home, and a handful of subdivisions built from the 1950s through the 1990s. Within the circle was wooded land close to wild, suburban lawns, remnant farm fields, surviving pastures, strip malls, mini-marts, mill village yards, and a golf course. I'd etched a circle around some of the richest people in Spartanburg and some of its poorest, and every level in between. And a creek runs through it, tying it all together. On both sides of the creek is a wide, wild, and impressive flood-plain, "the big sediment trap," Terry Ferguson unromantically calls it.

The first thing I did to alter the map was to color in the flood-plain up to the one-hundred-year flood line with an aquama-rine marker. When I finished, it looked like a lake had been cre-ated from the mill village of Glendale a mile upstream. When it was filled in we were some of the lucky ones: lakefront property!

Flood frequency along a creek or river is a probability state-ment based on topography, climate, weather, and records of stream flow. The frequency is a measure of how high the prob-ability is that a piece of land will be flooded in a year, in fifty years, a hundred years, even in five hundred years. A seasonal flood, once or twice a year, is smaller than the one-hundred-year flood insurance maps are most concerned with.

Records haven't been kept on Lawson's Fork for very long, so we don't really know if a one-hundred-year flood has pushed through anytime in recent history. We do know that "periodi-cally a great deal of water comes down a creek or river," as Terry likes to say. "That's normal. A floodplain is an active part of the river that just doesn't always have water in it," Terry says after a hard rain, when he drives me up to the bridge on Lake For-est Drive for a dose of scientific confirmation. That bridge is almost due west of us, near the outer edge of the circle. When the river floods Terry walks out to the middle of the concrete bridge and listens to the water coursing only a few feet below. I look upstream toward town and downstream toward our house and see the muddy acres of flood reclaiming the bottomland fields under the big transmission lines.

Terry's quite righteous about such things as floods and justly so. At least once a year Lawson's Fork Creek spreads out into its big flat floodplain, and we get to see it. These periodic natural disasters give Terry's geologist spirit great satisfaction. He uses these events to talk about the dynamics of watersheds and point out the awful choices developers often made before communities like ours began to see the disadvantages of building in a one-hundred-year flood zone.

Standing on the bridge Terry points upstream on the west bank to where a home-owner recently built. "He's clearly in the floodplain," Terry says. "Someday he'll have to say hello to the creek in his basement."

Among the residents of the watershed there were a few other friends I already knew I'd have to go exploring with who would give me different points of view—builder Manning Lynch, who lives over on the country club ridge across from us; retired professor B. G. Stephens, who grew up downstream in Glendale; and Fred Parrish, who has lived much of his life near the circle. I knew there would be others, but this was a good start.

So that January morning I etched my circle on the map, it became a sort of imaginary bull's eye to work out from on foot or by bike, car, or boat, and also a metaphor to draw me back toward home when I wandered too far out of the circle.

The world isn't really a map, and it's not made up of circles, and none of us really lives in the center of anything. The Copernican Revolution settled all that, we've been told, no matter what *Black Elk Speaks* claims about Harney Peak being the center of the universe. So why backslide? Why throw everything modern and boundless out of kilter and set about to put some out-of-the-way place like a spot on the east side of Spartanburg, South Carolina, in the center of a circle again?

Part of the plan was arbitrary. Betsy's old chipped white saucer was round and limited in size, and at the moment it seemed the right thing to do. I had time, and I needed focus in our new home for a month of free exploration, and I wanted a project to fill out the days so that I wouldn't waste them. But I also wanted some sort of limit on what I needed to learn, and a saucer's diameter didn't seem overwhelming.

Settling can have a variety of meanings: to appoint, to fix, to resolve definitely and conclusively, to place, to close an account, to colonize, to establish a way of life or a business, to get quiet, to calm down, to bring to rest, to secure (as in a title or a legal process), to decide, arrange, or agree, to pay a bill, to clear (as in liquid), to sink down gradually, to dispose of fully, to put in a place of rest.

Maps, definitions, and notes are helpful, but in the end there is a danger I'll simply be left with only nice metaphors and a large pile of notes, what any historian would call "research material" but no real story. The story of this place will have to be found within so much more. I'm no historian, so my story can never be simply what I find in libraries, archives, and interviews. The real story, the one I'm interested in, is always out there somewhere among the hills and floodplain, along the creek, in the lives of the plants and animals and people that cross paths with me when I walk the land. But the story is also within me, flowing outward from my life, my memories, and my perception of things.

If life is a circle and not a line, then at fifty, I'm unsettlingly far around the perimeter of my circle from where I started. Five years earlier when I was forty-five it wasn't so certain that at this milestone I would be settled at all. There was no guarantee I would be married, or in a new house, and with a new family. Some friends note my late settlement and are disappointed. They liked the former me, the "forever young" poet on the road, endlessly traveling. My settlement shows that person climbed in the backseat years ago, replaced at the wheel by the one I have become. "Touring the world / tilling a small field to its limits," a Japanese haiku poet once wrote. For the last three years my particular field has been this circle, two miles wide and round like the moon.

That January morning I drew the circle, I had a fire burning in the big living room with the high ceiling. Each round tossed on the hearth reminded me of the real price of settlement. When they cleared our house site the bulldozer operator left a pile of red oak for me to split, and we've burned that wood day by day, and have been now for three winters.

I've worked here mornings ever since to split open and spark the story of this place and our settlement here. I've walked out and back many times between the creek and the house, between settlement and the freedom I felt before I came here to live. My explorations have taken the form of those two stories—settlement and freedom—both with their own comforts.

This narrative is finally beginning to feel like one story—my life, Betsy's, the boys watching television downstairs, the suburbs, the forest, the creek, and the floodplain outside our windows. As I type in the study, Apple Cider's intensity has faded a little, but the sun still warms my back. Today it's just cleared the gray wall our architects designed to pierce the house down the middle and support our lives and the triangular decks on the house's backside. Our designers, unlike most, actually cared about the path of the sun and placed our house on the lot according to it. Our heating bill reflects that care, less than what a house our size should cost.

For twenty years I lived like a stream in flood, and only for the last decade have I begun to rest comfortably. I've sat for three years here exploring the real landscape of home, but I've also reexamined a few of the remembered landscapes, places, and people that have returned and swirled like storm water into the current.

In the floodplain below our yard the creek moves quietly along its ancient bed. It gushes over fallen trees and cuts slowly even now at the sediment laid down each time the creek floods. We humans have no emotional FEMA map to show us where or when we should and should not build.

The other day I told Terry Ferguson I was trying to finish up my book about settlement, and he thought I said "sediment." He said very seriously, "Just watch the creek. It can teach you all there is to know about sediment. Just watch and listen."

Only in the past few generations and only in a handful of cultures have people claimed to need houses. Now almost all of us have houses, but most of us are still homeless.

RICHARD MANNING, *A Good House: Building a Life on the Land*

How We Came to Live Here

When we decided to get married three years ago, Betsy and I also decided to build. Separate households would be disbanded and real estate liquidated, creating enough equity to finance our dream house. We were both in our forties and lucky to have found each other. We had been married to others before, but neither union lasted as long as the vows promised. My first marriage was very short in duration, less than a year. Betsy's endured much longer and was of much more consequence. After seventeen years, when the marriage finally ended, Betsy had two fine boys, Rob and Russell, to show for it. Twenty years after mine dissolved, I had less to show—just a set of divorce papers filed safely away and two decades of unsettled freedom.

Working through this freedom kept me single for twenty years and often on the road. I like to dream, and during those two decades my dreams were much more interesting to me than my grounding realities. Being a dreamer was a good excuse to avoid a steady job, to keep from marrying, from committing to anything. "You need to own your fear of commitment," a girlfriend once said to me. It was not a good moment in the relationship, which ended soon afterward. "Can't I rent the feeling for a few more years?" I asked as a parting compromise. But things change, even people who are so paralyzed that they need the iron lung of infinite possibility to breathe.

Frank Lloyd Wright, quite a dreamer himself, says in *The Natural House* that when selecting a habitation site there is always the question of how close to the city you should be. Get as far out as you can, Wright advised in 1954. "Avoid the suburbs— dormitory towns—by all means." Go, he said, way out in the country, and "when others follow, as they will . . . move on."

The answer as to how far out you can move, Wright claims, depends on what kind of slave you are. What kind of slaves, I of course asked, are we? I'd never thought of myself as enslaved, but I admire Frank Lloyd Wright, and I had to consider just what he might mean. After all, I am a southerner, so the word "slave" has some serious baggage.

Wright did not have my personal history or the entire history of the South in mind when he talked about slaves. By slavery he meant whatever it is that "employs" you can also most likely enslave you. After thinking through Wright's terms of "employment" it began to occur to me that I am now fully enslaved—to my car, this house, the college where I work, even to my sense of who I am: writer, poet, teacher, environmentalist. All of these masters contributed to determining where we would build.

Our jobs, as enslavements, are not the worst the area has to offer, and at least they promise flexible hours and adequate income. Betsy and I are both writers as well, and I struggle, in particular, to write imaginatively about the natural world around me, and that effort often seems to enslave my every moment. "At home in the world," Sam Hamill, a poet friend of mine, once called a book of his essays. I've worked twenty-five years to understand what he meant by that.

Until the last few years, I didn't need much in the way of home, and I was skeptical of those who did. I lived by the code of the wandering poet for twenty years, but love has a way of rewriting personal codes, so when Betsy and I decided to get married, there was never any question I would take the challenges of settlement straight on. Throughout history, from hut to condominium, the path of settlement has always passed through some form of structure-building and occupation. Slave to a mortgage? When we said, "I do," we both accepted this mutual obligation that stretched thirty years into the future.

Wright would say that our particular sort of slavery (writing, teaching, editing) would not necessarily place us close to town, because writers can live anywhere. But Wright's anywhere is not an option for us. We have become slaves of another sort, to our love for this place, a South Carolina piedmont city, and the creek that runs through it. Because of our love for Lawson's Fork of the Pacolet River, we wanted to live on it. It was always just a question of where.

When we started to talk of settlement we pulled out the Spartanburg County map and looked at all the possibilities. Northwest of town, close to the foot of the Blue Ridge, the landscape is more dramatic, but Lawson's Fork is too small up there to offer much appeal—maybe five to ten feet wide, running through old farm fields and new cookie-cutter subdivisions, the "sprawl" of the last decade. But by the time the creek passes through the city of Spartanburg it begins to take on the presence of a river— up to thirty feet across—and it begins to meander through its big floodplain.

Much of the land southeast of town is in this big floodplain and therefore unsuitable for building, trapped in real-estate limbo by regulation and periodic flooding. The land on the few ridges that pinch in close to the creek is already "built-out," because sprawl in the sixties and seventies crawled east for a mile or two before stalling, hard up against a mill village and the line of the neighboring school district that the settlers of that generation had deemed undesirable. The creek takes a hard southern bend down there and wiggles a time or two before plunging over a dramatic series of small waterfalls called Glendale's Upper and Lower Shoals. Downstream from Glendale the stubborn rural landscape of South Carolina takes over for good, and there isn't much in the way of sprawl before the creek's confluence with the Pacolet River four miles away. This, we knew, would be the landscape of our future: the east side of Spartanburg, what Betsy calls "the Lower East Side."

We considered taking Wright's advice and getting way out of town, toying around with building on some wild land that Betsy's brother owns on the lower stretches of Lawson's Fork off Emma Cudd Road, a long-wooded ridge high above the creek. We revved up our dreams to the level of fantasy and for a moment imagined building that far from town, but the reality of daily chores wet that fantasy down like a summer storm. Did we really want to drive ten miles into town several times a day? Rural life sounds good, but the complex reality of forgotten groceries and transportation to soccer and basketball practice for our two early teen boys was more than we could tackle. We, upon consideration, admitted we were slaves to all our own scheduling.

We also considered staying near downtown Spartanburg on the stately ridge above Lawson's Fork, in the old neighborhood called Converse Heights, where Betsy already owned a home when we started going out. Once farmland on the edge of town, this streetcar suburb was founded in 1906, and it's full of early twentieth-century homes. It's where many of Spartanburg's prominent citizens once lived or still do live, including Thomas Wolfe's brother Fred, two former governors, a former U.S. secretary of state, the former head of the New York Philharmonic, and the current mayor. Many in Spartanburg have projected their domestic dreams there and watched them rise in wood and brick.

Betsy raised her two boys in Converse Heights, on Palmetto

Street, in another time, another marriage, and so it's a place dense with memory for her. She'd spent her childhood on her grandmother's front porch on Mills Avenue and played in the park down the street.

Settling in Converse Heights bothered me though. In high school I drove home every day through the neighborhood, but I never remember thinking, "You know, I'd like to live here some day." I found an odd comfort among the ranches and split-levels one more ring of suburban sprawl further out. I always wanted to live in a brick ranch house, not one of those one-hundred-year-old wood mansions with abandoned servants' entrances and yardmen. I was always a little uncomfortable with the neighborhood's strict sense of order and its one-note socioeconomics, though I know Converse Heights is what all the new developers are working for in "the New Urbanism"—traditional houses on small lots, front porches, sidewalks, little parks remodeled from basketball courts to playgrounds for the toddlers of yet another generation of Spartanburg's professional class.

There was an upside to the neighborhood's stable prosperity that Betsy had cultivated—property values were high, so when Betsy pulled up stakes she was able to cart away some equity to help finance our dream house.

So we looked for a lot somewhere along the creek, but not in Converse Heights. We wanted to be near some wildness, and we knew if there is wildness near the city of Spartanburg, it is to be found in this long expanse of floodplain downstream from Converse Heights. Almost a half-mile wide in places, this low, periodically wet territory continues for almost four miles, all the way to the old mill village of Glendale. Only three pedestrian and four auto bridges cross it in that distance. On the upstream end of the floodplain, near Spartanburg High School, seventy acres were acquired in the 1980s by SPACE, the Spartanburg Area Conservancy, and there they maintain miles of public trails winding through escaped Chinese privet, English ivy, and planted pine, native river birch, and river cane.

A mile downstream the creekside trail abruptly ends, and from there on to the next bridge at Lake Forest Drive it's a linear mix of parcels of private land—the weedy butt ends of low-lying backyards, wealthy people's back forties, the margins of two condo developments—and it's off limits to the public unless you're in a boat. It's always been the dream of many who walk the SPACE trail south along the creek to keep going downstream, but the reality of walking there has rubbed up hard against other people's deed-backed desires.

Below the bottleneck of private ownership, the floodplain really opens out. In the 1920s a dairy called Springdale grew corn in the bottoms there, owned by early textile magnate Victor Montgomery. The dairy persisted until the early sixties. Now thick hardwoods have grown up in the bottomland where the cows once grazed and the corn once grew. Not many in town even know the dairy existed. Its presence has been mentioned in several local history books, but few now think of dairy cows when they drive east down Lake Forest Drive toward Lawson's Fork, their route passing near the site of the old barns.

The Country Club of Spartanburg was built in 1908 on a high ridge on the north side of the creek, below the dairy. Back then the land the club converted from farmland really was in the country, and you could even take a trolley out to play golf. The land further downstream on the country club side of the creek is home to Spartanburg's largest sewer treatment plant, the club's neighbor since 1938. Spartanburg was one of the earliest cities in South Carolina to treat its sewage, even though "treatment" back then simply consisted of pumping raw sewage into settling ponds, disposing of the sludge, and then directing the wastewater (what is called effluent) back into the creek. Some say the dairy used the sewage sludge as fertilizer on their fields, and I like to imagine those early textile magnates on the club's front nine catching a whiff of natural fertilizer and the sewer plant's primary processes as they putted out on number seven.

Old soil survey aerial photos show that the floodplain of Lawson's Fork below Lake Forest Drive was farmland as late as 1970. The bulk of this fertile bottomland along the creek is now owned by the country club and by the Pierce family. There is no visible boundary between the club's property and the larger Pierce tract downstream. Together these two tracts form a mature forest of impressive proportions—maybe three hundred acres total. The fate of this wild tract is tied now to the country club and the Pierce clan.

The country club is a private institution with a board that changes periodically, and because of that, it's hard to know what will happen to their land. We're not members of the club, and so what we know of their plans comes secondhand from friends who are. We want to see it preserved as green space, but we don't own it, and so far there has been no successful effort on the part of club members to save the land from development.

The Pierce land has been controlled by three generations— grandfather Tom, his son Tommy, and now Tommy's children. Born in Iowa in 1901, Tom Pierce started work by the time he was fourteen. Soon after, as a very young man, Pierce made his way east to Virginia, and there he became the manager of a dairy. By 1927 he was painting cars in a Ford assembly plant in Norfolk, and from there, came south to Spartanburg to work for the Burwell Chevy dealership downtown. It's said Burwell brought Pierce in to run his paint shop, and it took young Tom Pierce two days to get from Charlotte to Spartanburg because the roads were so bad. He arrived in Spartanburg with one suit of clothes and two camel-hair paintbrushes in his pockets.

What Tom Pierce found when he arrived from Norfolk was a small southern county seat ringed by cotton fields and peach trees and isolated mill villages. By 1937 that ambitious young man had acquired Spartanburg's Ford dealership, and for the next thirty years Pierce Motor Company supplied the forward-looking Tom Pierce cash to buy the cheap county land that ringed the growing "sun-belt" city.

By the forties and fifties Tom Pierce had bought and traded his way into east-side real estate in a big way, acquiring land all along Lawson's Fork east of town. Pierce even bought Victor Montgomery's Springdale Dairy in the late fifties, and about the same time added an old farm on the north side of the creek. These tracts would become the subdivisions known to-day as Pierce Acres and Lake Forest Hills. Pierce sold off the ridge tops for lots, but the large bottomland acreage along the creek remained undeveloped and covered with mature hard-wood through the end of the last century and into the present one. He kept the dairy going until the midsixties, milking 150 to 200 cows right up until the end. Today the dairy is gone, but you can still find the Springdale Dairy milk bottles for sale on eBay.

In 1958 Pierce began cutting the roads for Pierce Acres on our side of the creek and planning the subdivision along the high east/west ridge top. Pierce took advantage of his Ford product line to name the streets—Fairlane, Mustang, Galaxy, Taurus, Maverick, Torino, Pinto, Courier, Starline, and our own Tempo Court. Soon after the roads were cut, the Ford dealer-turned-land-speculator sold the raw development to a Tryon, North Carolina, corporation. When the houses went on the market in the early sixties the subdivision filled up quickly with young professionals freshly relocated to this textile town in a growth spurt. Jerry Richardson, now owner of the Carolina Pan-thers, and his early business partner Charlie Bradshaw, both members of the South Carolina Business Hall of Fame, had starter homes there.

When Tom Pierce died in 1968, he left the dealership and

his real estate interests to his son, Tommy. In hindsight Tom Pierce looks like a real estate visionary of his time. Did Pierce foresee Spartanburg sprawling east before finally lurching, subdivision by subdivision, back west toward Greenville? Or did he just love old farmland and see it as a safe investment sometime on down the line? It's because of the Pierces that so much of the land along this stretch of the creek remains wooded and undeveloped today.

One thing's for sure: Tom Pierce knew the moods of the creek that formed one of old Springdale Dairy's borders. Lawson's Fork rises fast and floods wide down in the area known as The Flats, so building in this broad floodplain is foolhardy. Landowners with good sense, like the Pierces, have been limited as to what they could do in the floodplain. Logging, agricultural, and recreation are all human activities that seem strong matches with the unpredictable moods of the creek.

The Pierces use the floodplain as a private hunting preserve, complete with a scattering of deer stands and duck ponds. One of the largest open tracts near the city is the Pierce parcel on the south bank, a stretch of cleared bottom below the sewer plant where the creek takes a big bend. They still plow this section every spring and plant it in corn and turnips for the deer and turkey they hunt. It's probably the last active agricultural parcel on the creek close to town, a surviving remnant of Spartanburg's (and the Pierces') deep farming history.

There is one more player in our east-side development game along the creek: the Milliken family. On both sides of the creek below the Pierce and country club properties "the Milliken tract" covers over two hundred acres of bottomland and recently logged ridge tops. Owned quietly for decades by the local textile family, the tract is a small piece within the network and vast puzzle of their South Carolina landholdings. It's a jewel they may not even be aware exists beyond entries on a tax sheet; there are two good-sized tributary creeks and a shoals. Much of

Spartanburg County's history has crisscrossed the land there. The Old Georgia Road, a colonial road, forded Lawson's Fork at the shoals, and an early ironworks forged metal in the vicinity for the Revolution.

Downstream from the Milliken family parcel the terrain gets steep and closes around the creek, and Terry's sediment trap disappears. Just past the Milliken land is the old Glendale Mill site, and another SPACE preserve, this one thirteen acres. The two SPACE preserves, four river miles apart and separated by undeveloped floodplain and private land, form the anchors for what could one day be an unbroken "green corridor," a linear creekside expanse of close to one thousand acres, stretching from near downtown out into the country.

When Betsy lived in Converse Heights, we'd walk on the public SPACE trails and dream our way down into the big, wide creek bottom toward where we now live. That upper SPACE preserve was our nearby wilderness where we might find morel mushrooms, cross paths with a black rat snake, sight a weasel, or spot a redheaded woodpecker in a wetland where a lodge of beavers had backed up a small creek. The wildness we sensed up there was the main reason we fell in love with the idea of building on the creek. It was while walking that urban trail in the bottomland that we began to hope someday the community might first recognize and then protect this unbroken expanse all the way from Converse Heights downstream to Glendale. The piedmont might not have any national parks, but it could have a Lawson's Fork Preserve.

Sometimes I feel a little guilty about all this dreaming. What rights do people like me have to dream about other people's property? Thoreau did it though, in *Wild Fruits*—"I think that not only the channel, but one or both banks of every river should be a public highway, for a river is not useful merely to float on . . . one bank might have been reserved as a public walk and the trees that adorned it have been protected, and frequent avenues have been provided leading to it from the main street. This would have cost but few acres of land and but little wood, and we should have been gainers by it."

In my own reveries I too rush rudely among the acres of my neighbors. It's only recently that it occurred to me my dreams might collide with the dreams of others. As Gaston Bachelard says in *The Poetics of Space*, a major benefit of a house is it's a place for daydreaming, a place people can dream in peace. Bachelard might have seen a house as a good place for daydreaming, but in the poetics of space the moment your dreams step across property lines you can be charged with trespassing, the property rights' equivalent of disturbing the peace.

So should we even dream of protection and wildness of other people's land or simply keep our own scrap of grass and trees tidy? These questions led us to buying land right in the middle of what we hoped would someday be a protected corridor along the creek. The preserve didn't exist yet on anybody's map but ours. Of course we hoped—yeah, we even dreamed—it someday would.

Our house is our corner of the world.

GASTON BACHELARD, *The Poetics of Space*

Dream House / Green House

After a few months of searching, Betsy found our Lawson's Fork lot about two miles downstream from Converse Heights, on the north side of the creek, in a three-street, almost empty subdivision called Forest Hills. "Forest Hills?" friends always ask. "That's not a subdivision, it's a tennis tournament."

Poking out the backside of Pierce Acres, Mustang Drive forms the Forest Hills main drag before dead-ending in the floodplain. People get lost trying to find it, even people who know Spartanburg. Laid out as a circular farm track by Tom Pierce in 1965, the Forest Hills roads weren't paved until the late 1980s, and the covenants weren't established until 1989. Yes, Spartanburg's Forest Hills does exist, but it somehow defies UPS tracking and MapQuest.

Why did all these lots sit unsold for a quarter century? Was the answer geographic? The land is forested, but it is also, as the name implies, hilly, and it requires a great deal of site work. Wright says that the best kind of land to buy is flat since it's cheaper to build on.

Could another problem also be the presence of the city's sewer plant located only a quarter of a mile upstream? Betsy, a former business editor, felt the explanation was most likely economic. Since the 1980s, most of the growth in Spartanburg has headed west. The demand was to the west, and no matter how many suitable building lots were available east of town they would most likely go unpurchased. Betsy has a nose for such economic practicalities, and I always see issues a little differently once she weighs in.

But in spite of economic practicalities and our lack of neighbors, we decided to build on Tempo Court, just off Mustang Drive. We had the cul-de-sac completely to ourselves and joked about buying all three lots and changing the road's name to LeSabre Court, or better yet, Park Avenue, since Betsy's family owns the Buick dealership in town. Our closest neighbors were three lots away on one side, and outside the entrance to Forest Hills on the other. It was fine with us. We liked the privacy.

These are requirements for residence that would have baffled most real estate agents—no neighbors and no certainty of them in the future. If "location, location, location" is the first law of real estate, then we had violated it. And if that wasn't enough, our early construction estimates were about to violate another sacred creed of the business—never build (or own) the most expensive house in the neighborhood.

We had a favorite architect, Fraser Pajak, a design professor at nearby Converse College. He'd given up his private practice to concentrate on a teaching career, but I knew that in the 1970s and 1980s he'd designed three or four of the most interesting houses in the county. Fraser is medium height and stout like a terrier. He has more enthusiasm for carving up space into livable stretches than anyone could imagine. All his houses are modern, designed from the inside out, and turn their back on the "period" styles so common to the subdivisions constantly springing up in Spartanburg. His houses are all a little funky—often angular—but very livable. We called and asked him to take on our project. He agreed to meet with us at the coffee-house downtown, though up front he had to tell us that he could not "draw" our house since he did not possess the modern computer program called Auto CAD (computer assisted design) used to create elevations and floor plans. We would have to work with HP Architects, a firm in town he was associated with, for that. He would come up with the concept and another architect, Bob Bourguigon, one of South Carolina's then rare LEED (Leaders in Energy and Environmental Design) certified "green" designers, would take it from there.

At that first meeting we told Fraser what Thoreau had said in *Wild Fruits*, that most homeowners are still related "to our native fields as the navigator to undiscovered islands in the sea." We didn't want to feel that way. We wanted an architect to design a place where we could settle, become natives to this place. The design should be "green," with an open floor plan less than three thousand square feet. We didn't want anything that looked like the "McMansions" that were popping up in the up-scale neighborhoods around town. We were taken with a series of books—the *Not So Big House* series, and it was in them we found many of the concepts that became the basis for Fraser and Bob's design.

Part of our deal with our sons Rob and Russell for our getting married was that they would acquire their own rooms and entertainment space in the new house, so we also set Fraser to work to figure out a basement design that would suit the ways of two teenage boys. Rob was already fifteen when we started this project. He was a little more difficult to pull in. "Whatever," was his response to buying the wooded lot on the creek. As for design, when we said "sustainable," his only major concern was that we did not plan to build a house that looked like a hunting lodge or a scout hut. "You know, logs," he said. "No logs."

When Fraser and Bob returned with their first "concept" drawings, Fraser illustrated what he wanted "her" to look like by bending at the waist, throwing one arm back at an odd, shoulder separating angle, and the other out straight. "This is the shape of her floor plan," he said. "She's like a ship at full sail into the wind." We trusted his intuition. What it translated into when we saw the first drawings was a house with a large bend, like a flying V tucked into the hillside. There was a tall concrete block wall through the middle as well. We stood by, as Wright had said most of his early clients did, "interested and excited, but way beyond their means." We knew we were off on a great adventure, and we were scared to death how much it was going to cost.

But we were committed. One November afternoon after we had bought our lot and signed a contract with our architects, we took Russell out to see it. We brought along our dogs Toby and Ellie Mae as well. Russell, twelve at the time, had hauled his mountain bike out of the garage and thrown it in my truck bed. We explained to him that there was a trail downstream along the creek. It was private property but we knew neighborhood people who walked there every day. Russell dropped down off the ridge and took off downstream on the trail next to the creek. He was headed for "the upper shoals." Betsy and I stood on the knoll top on our lot and looked down into the big floodplain and caught the creek sparkling through the bare hardwoods in the direction of where the boy and the dogs had disappeared. We were standing just to the west of where our house would soon break ground. I bent down and picked up three pieces of worked quartz, one obviously a notched and stemmed atlatl point, maybe as much as seven or eight thousand years old. I explained to Betsy about the ancient spear thrower that was in use before the bow and arrow. "It's a good sign," she said. "Other people have settled here and enjoyed the view."

In ten minutes Russell came back, trailing the dogs. He looked like he'd seen a ghost. "I was riding along and I thought I heard Toby coming up beside me. When I turned, a deer was running even with me," Russell explained. "I said, 'ahhh!' and it veered off into the woods." It was another good habitation sign. We now keep the quartz point and the skull of a white-tailed deer in the living room, talismans for our settlement.

In late December of 2001 we broke ground. We invited twenty friends to the hillside, cooked hot dogs, and asked two minister friends to come out and bless the spot. Beth Ely, the Episcopal priest who would marry us, offered an Anglican prayer. Meg Barnhouse, a Unitarian, showed up with two ceremonial rattles and a sage bundle. She chanted and offered the burning sage to the four cardinal directions over the house site. By the time the bulldozer took down the hardwoods where the house was to stand we had our bases covered, both pagan and Christian.

Fraser and Bob began work with great care designing a sustainable house, not always an easy chore in South Carolina. The floor plan they produced showed a structure that operated by its own particular set of rules. The design had some of Wright's Prairie School in it, some Arts and Crafts style, and some elements all of its own. It would be easy and efficient to heat and cool. It had the openness we'd hoped for, took advantage of the site, and had well-designed placement of numerous opening windows for ventilation. The materials were natural wood, block, and gypsum board. There was no way to look at the plan for the house on its wooded lot and not think of it as an intermediate space between the human realm and the natural world beyond.

When construction began, HP Architects, the firm Bob and Fraser work for, put a big sign out front advertising its "sustainable design," and for two years John Bell Hines, the firm's owner, had a picture of our house in the window of his office downtown. It felt at times like we were really doing something revolutionary with our choice of a house in Spartanburg. HP's design racks up enough points so that it could be LEED certified if the process had been, at the time, available for residential construction. We're still proud of our sustainable choices: rapidly renewable bamboo flooring, recycled newspaper insulation, low VOC (volatile organic compounds) paints and stains, low-flow toilets, recycling area in the pantry, recycling of construction debris.

The contractor, however, didn't take as much care as the architects, so the process of getting into the house was painful, fraught with delay and sloppy workmanship that had to be corrected all along the way. The only builder we could afford was quite traditional, and it seemed to us he was quickly in over his head with this unusual house. In order to cut costs he hired a framing crew that made us often think we'd fallen into *The Twilight Zone*. They were right out of the 1970s, a ragged remnant crew that had worked for the contractor's father in that long-ago decade. They still hammered nails because modern tools like nail guns were out of the crew's tight budget. We laugh and brag that we probably have the last custom home built in South Carolina where a nail gun was not used to frame and finish every square inch.

In November of 2002, what we originally thought would be the month we could move into our house, we drove to Bill and Kristin Taylor's house on Emma Cudd Road. At 11 a.m. our priest friend Beth married us in the front yard, with the roar of Lawson's Fork's Glendale Shoals nearby. It was so cold that day Betsy had to wear a knee-length wool coat. The boys and two witnesses looked on when we both said, "I do." That night we met friends at Cleveland Park on the north side of town. We danced to bluegrass and ate barbeque. Hardly anyone wore a suit. Marriage is a flood, but it's usually the first step in the long mile along the road to settlement as well. For our honeymoon we drove away to the mountains, up beyond where our creek begins. It's good to get some perspective on things at the start of something.

Ten months over schedule, the contractor finally drowned in the details of the collapsing project, and the architects had to hire someone else to finish the job. There were moments when we wished we had bought one of those neo-French floor plans off the shelf, a house with a steeply pitched hipped roof and round or arched windows.

Finding subcontractors to install our unusual or "green" materials was not always easy either, but afterward the choices made for good stories. The floor man said he could work with bamboo, but his crew appeared and disappeared like fog on the creek. He ran out of materials three times and avoided our questions about whether numerous nail holes could ever be patched. He raged at the contractor about uneven subflooring, and the contractor raged at him about his crew's uncertain schedule. The crew—two locals with mullets and jeans that somehow hooked on bony hips an inch or so before they plummeted to the floor—listened to heavy metal and inched through the house on kneepads, installing a product they'd never heard of before we asked for it.

Our concrete countertops were manufactured on site by a longhaired art major in a silk shirt whose last name was Miracle. He camped in the house for days, ate turkey sub sandwiches, and strutted around the construction site complaining about the noise. "I'm a concrete artist!" he screamed at the floor crew. To finish the project he covered his silk shirt in overalls, pulled on a gas mask fit for nuclear war and sanded and sealed the lovely concrete surface he'd created.

We moved into the basement in May of 2003, after almost two years of construction. It was Betsy who'd had enough and pushed it through. She simply said, "We're coming," and on May 1 we moved. It would take another six weeks before the new contractor finished the upstairs enough for us to move in entirely and acquire a certificate of occupancy.

The day the movers arrived with our furniture, a five-foot

black rat snake was curled up sunning on the rear concrete patio. I moved it back down into the floodplain, and within an hour it returned, staking claim to one of the premier sites for reptile thermoregulation on the lower east side. Betsy saw this visitation as ominous. I greeted it as if our wild spirits in the floodplain had brought us a housewarming gift. That first night, screens firmly in place, we left the windows open.

It rained twenty-one inches that spring. Everything was sodden, and the creek was high. It came out of its banks three times, and we could see it standing in the woods below the unfinished house. There were seepages everywhere, springs popping out of the hillsides around us. The water table was full, and it felt like we'd somehow been transported to a real rain forest. It was a bumper year for frogs. In the creek bottom below us I could hear cricket, leopard, bull, chorus, and green and gray tree frogs, all crying out for love.

For six weeks we had one working toilet in the house, no cable, no shower, no hot water, and we brushed our teeth with a hose on the patio. Our possessions were piled around us in moving boxes. Betsy and I slept in our double bed in a tiny "bonus room" behind the fireplace that wasn't even originally in the plans. There were no windows in it, and the block walls were all cold and clammy with moisture.

Our only relief was evenings when we'd order take-out Chinese for four, ascend our staircase with half its treads in place to the living room and out onto the unfinished deck above us, and dangle our feet off the edge and listen to the frogs.

How did the boys feel about the house? Of course they were annoyed that it wasn't finished on time and they had to drive to their grandfather's house to shower. Russell, almost fourteen when we moved in, had little to say, but he "nested" quicker than Rob—he taped the covers of old *Sports Illustrated* magazines and Carolina Panthers posters to the walls and slid his bed around the room until he found exactly the right place for it.

Rob, sixteen when we occupied the basement, was struck first by the house's beauty. One night, sitting on the deck, out of nowhere he commented on how much he loved our new place—the sounds, the space. "It's more like a work of art than a house," he said, looking up at the big decorative block wall holding up the deck.

I noticed the beauty too, but I was pulled outside where the honeysuckle was blooming. All that first month I looked to it for strength. The honeysuckle was everywhere out in the creek bottom, and its sweet scent of the nectar I'd sucked out as a piedmont child proceeded it. The persistent vine somehow always found the light, and it bloomed. I know Japanese honeysuckle is a hated "alien species," but it seemed so at home in this place, and that comfort was something I thought I could learn from it. I too was an alien to this process of settlement, but it felt so right, and it worked for the honeysuckle. Besides, the deer love it, and Betsy loves having the deer around.

Within a week in the basement, I had my first dream in the new house, not about wild honeysuckle but about a plant associated for centuries with love and domesticity. We are in a garden somewhere, Betsy and I, and we see a beautiful ancient rose and love its color and want to transplant it. So I snip, snip on the runners and Betsy says no, I have to cut it nearer the roots where the stalk is thick if I want to propagate. So I move down the stalk and try to cut it there. When I slice in with the sheers it feels like meat, like cutting into freshly roasted turkey breast, and the whole plant starts falling apart and I try to stick it back together again but can't.

There's so much of the anxiety of settlement in that dream—wanting to take the beauty of the domestic rose with me, yet failing. And what of the turkey breast? Maybe it was a not-so-veiled reference to the house we were building as a "turkey," or was it more serious than that? Of course there's something of the "raw and the cooked" in the dream. "It was cooked turkey breast?" a friend asked when I repeated the dream. "It wasn't red meat?" Perhaps this dream was an early settlement warning: leave the ancient rose alone, let it grow where it's happiest and give up the desire to move it. I took the dream to mean I should plant other things. There are no roses in the gardens we've planted around the house.

When the contractor finally finished in late June of 2003 the house was something we moved easily into—unpacking boxes and arranging furniture upstairs—and fell in love with immediately. It looked like nothing in the neighborhood and, if it were not tucked back in the hardwoods on a deserted out-of-the-way cul-de-sac, it would probably be a tourist attraction of some questionable sort. "The Teter-Lane folly," the more fiscally faint of heart might call it. You know the type, those more interested in resale than inspiration, whose idea of "southern living" comes directly out of the magazine by that name.

Our big gray block wall is made of a specialty concrete called blue stone, cast of sand and river gravel from right up the road in Asheville, so we think of it as a local product. A series of shed roofs conjoin with the wall at odd angles. The metal roof (what we call "piedmont vernacular") is so bright that any airline pilot flying from Atlanta to Charlotte could pick it out on a sunny day. We soaked our ship-lapped cypress siding, sustainably harvested in south Georgia, in bleaching oil and sealed it to help our house disappear into the woods. We've landscaped mostly with native plants, and there's a wildflower meadow over our septic field. Like that of an English Arts and Crafts house, our front yard is loose, overflowing, and natural. The mulch path to our front door meanders down two rough granite steps and over a wooden boardwalk set at an angle to the concrete stoop. There is no straight line from our curbside to the front door, no beeline walkway through a strictly ordered lawn. Instead, visiting us is more like a mini-outing to a wildlife preserve. There should be a kiosk at our drive rather than a mailbox.

Since we've built, several other lots in Forest Hills have sold, and two new houses have sprung up in the neighboring woods. The new neighbors have built more traditional houses with an eye toward resale. Our house grows more unique with each addition. Now, three years later, we've come to call it "Falling-water on a budget," and that's not far from wrong. Frank Lloyd Wright would recognize his spirit in Fraser and Bob's design. It's organic. It has a sense of unity. Everyone who visits says it matches our personalities, a little edgy and artsy, built with no regard for the safe rules of resale value in a town dominated by such values.

Our wide-open interior is filled with art, books, and light. There are thirty-nine big windows on the back walls, a southern exposure, and by choice we've applied no window treatments. There are dozens of patterns of light cast on the floors and walls as the sun moves from east to west through the seasons. The house rests comfortably on the slope above the Lawson's Fork floodplain, and out back someone would have to climb a tree to see in. "My heart keeps open house," the poet Theodore Roethke wrote in his poem by that name, "Open House." "My doors are widely swung." I think about Roethke when I walk though our house in the midday sun. I also think of the parable of the glass house and our differences with our neighbors' housing values and try not to throw too many stones.

Tomorrow I will be changed. Somehow in the
next passage of light, I will shed reptilian skin and feel the
wind's friction again. Sparks will fly. It's a hope for the right
kind of fear, the kind that does not turn away.

KIM STAFFORD, *Having Everything Right*

Eugene

So what if I were set adrift again, swirling free from the comfort
we've built up around us here? What if my burrow caved in, my
comfortable nook collapsed? That was how I had felt when I
left my first marriage in Oregon in 1981. My first stab at commitment ended there, dead on arrival. When that brief marriage
failed, it was as if I had been thrown out of the first nest I ever
tried to build.

I used to be a worshiper of the front edge of experience, a
master of beginnings. My favorite time was always the first, the
Eden moments, the time of romance and adventure. I knew little on those trips into the wild of what it takes to get through the
middle of things, and on toward the end. Adolescence for me
lingered much too long. By the time I was approaching forty,
I had taken on few of the limiting factors that help you learn
to accept, to persevere: wife and children, home ownership,
insurance, tenure, dreams of retirement.

My first marriage had been so brief. I let the relationship

slip away soon after the ceremony. I wish I could say it was passion that undid the knot. It was more like opening a hand and watching something you had grasped lightly slip out of reach. Up until recently I had never held tight again, experiencing a series of twenty-eight-year-old girlfriends (my age when I divorced) as I grew a year older each time. One of my friends finally said, after another breakup, "John, if you keep this up you will always be an incident in some young woman's life."

I was also avoiding other sorts of commitments. "Never trust a man who doesn't own property," an economics professor said to me once. I owned no property. I preferred to rent. When, at thirty-four, I took a teaching job at the college I had graduated from in my hometown, I moved into a small basement rental apartment and out of the back of my truck. In this economics professor's paradigm I was not to be trusted, but this rental was a huge step for me. It was difficult to stay stable, and I only could maintain it for nine months. Each summer I bolted the door on the rental apartment and headed west, all my possessions once again in the back of my pickup.

I worked at the college on year-to-year contracts, with no tenure track, because I lacked an advanced degree. (I had started graduate programs three times, but unexpected adventures had always been more important than the closure of a degree.) Mostly, the college hired me because the dean knew I was a promising teacher, a writer of growing reputation, and a native son. So they took a chance on me.

Floating below the radar, I waited each spring to see if there would be a contract for the following fall. I taught well, but I wasn't really committed to the life of a teacher. I always imagined in the back of my mind that the luck bus would arrive at my corner: I would sell a novel or a screenplay, and daily work as a teacher would become a choice, not a necessity. And retirement? Back then, I was still young. Retirement wasn't even on the map, much less around the bend. There was something I was after in those commitmentless years. Familiar places were to be avoided. Home at best was a collection of books, a sleeping bag, or a borrowed bed.

I traveled on my instincts, and I wasn't lacking in ambition, but I knew that what I wanted each time I went "out there" was surprise, delight that comes from risk, and rapture.

Last summer I was back in the Pacific Northwest, in Eugene, Oregon, at an academic conference, the meeting of the Association for the Study of Literature and Environment. It's a biennial gathering of those interested in "nature and culture" and the strange seams and intersections the two make where they cross. I always know I can find my tribe there, hundreds of like-minded people who prefer to get off the trail, to watch the sky for signs, and wear more fleece than business suits.

I'd left Eugene twenty-five years before on a bus with seven dollars in my pocket, unemployed, broken, with no plan to survive, headed back to Spartanburg with my tail between my legs. I returned to Eugene this time alone on a plane, on vacation from a full-time teaching job, a marriage, a house, a family, and my full boat of responsibilities.

Betsy couldn't come to the conference, though she loves ASLE and wanted to see Oregon for the first time. She decided she had to stay in Spartanburg and guard the nest. She had our teenage sons to tend.

So my first afternoon in Eugene I was alone and flooded with memories of my brief time there. It caught me a little by surprise. I'd lived up the hill from the university with my wife Margaret in a tiny house and cycled down the main drag through the college every day. My first day back I was eating lunch there when Barry Lopez, an old friend, walked past. I had forgotten he still lived in town. In a moment Barry walked back and said, "John?" as if he too had seen a haunting from the past. He sat down, and we made plans to meet later, but we talked briefly about my living here once in the early eighties and what we were up to now. "That was several lifetimes ago," he said when I told him it felt strange to be back.

That afternoon, before the conference officially began, I met up with another friend, Dan, for what I hoped would be a relaxing reentry float down the Willamette River, a pleasant reintroduction to wild Eugene. After the conference Dan planned to meet his son for a canoe trip down the Missouri River. Dan's seventeen-foot We-no-nah canoe was brand new, and we decided that we'd break it in on the mild white water of the river running through downtown Eugene. When I was there before the only thing wild about my life was my marriage, so this trip I hoped would reorient me toward things that concerned me more these days—"mountains and rivers without end" as Northwest poet Gary Snyder calls the life I prefer—and Oregon has plenty of them.

We put in at the boat landing in Alton Baker Park and paddled the placid millrace a mile back upstream just past the Interstate 5 Bridge. There we portaged the lightweight canoe across a slender spit of land and entered the Willamette proper on a sandy beach.

Paddling the millrace through Alton Baker had brought back memories of running with my ex-wife, a marathoner, while we'd lived in town. Twenty-five years past we'd run the trails through the park, winding along the river for miles, crossing and recrossing the current on bike bridges.

As we ran she told me how at the Falmouth Road Race several years before the local marathoner celebrity Alberto Salazar had exhausted himself in victory, in the heat, and they had to wrap him in ice as a priest was asked to administer the last rites.

"How does he do it?" I asked, crossing a bike bridge near I-5 as we headed out along the Willamette River.

"It's his heart," she responded and pounded her chest. Of

course I thought of the failures of our hearts, wondered how much room there was in Salazar's, how much room in ours.

"They'll open Salazar's chest at death," I said. "And there it will sit in a nest of arteries: his huge heart, silent finally after a life of pushing."

"Sometimes a heart is just a heart," she said.

My body slumped, my pace lightened. I fell back.

"You're too sensitive," she smiled.

I was sensitive back then. Sensitive and romantic. But it was a romantic gesture on her part that had brought us to Eugene. A year earlier, after graduating from the University of Virginia, Margaret had signed with Nike. Nike had courted her as far back as high school, and she talked about it as if they were a suitor. Nike fit her romantic notions about commerce, so she signed the deal, and we moved from Virginia to Eugene soon after our wedding.

I remember how her shoe was untied, so she'd stopped to tie it, steaming in the cool air. I wanted to climb inside her heart and ride there for the rest of the run, to see if she loved me. Then I would know whether I should leave. I would smell it in her blood, salty and thin, as it circulated though her body on this run. I would hang there in her heart by my hands, like doing a pull-up, and wait for the message from her returning blood. Or I would ride there inside her in a small boat like a kayak. It was called a bloodstream, surely it must go some place, to some safe harbor where we could sit and talk honestly, safely for the first time in months. I would have to get tiny to ride though her bloodstream, but I was willing. Was she willing to let me in? Was her heart open? Had it grown large enough with all her running?

"You're not talking," I remember her saying. "Are you off in your head again?"

When she said that I always came back to my body. We pushed the pace a little. It was her run, though I went on it religiously too. I didn't want to spoil it. I was not a true convert, a believer like her. She kept strict notes on the number of miles she ran each day, and at what pace. Running logs stretching back for years. She could look back and know exactly how many miles she had run on Christmas Day 1978, and how fast. The gears of her body turned smoothly every morning, just like the morning before, the week before, the month before, as they had since junior high school.

All the routes we ran back then were measured, and she kept a list of them in her head. There was the morning route and afternoon route. My favorite morning route was across the river, for five miles through the second-growth timber along wood chip trails. I liked the smell of the crushed fir pulp and bark, the smell of northwestern wood-rot and fungus growth that is still everywhere in Eugene.

Things break down. Living things break down in the damp air. Maybe rotting wood and fungus are horrible things to remember a marriage by, but I can't deny that smell.

"I like it on this trail because it smells like wood-rot," I remember finally saying one day, trying to be poetic.

"I like it because it's flat," Margaret said.

The Willamette was wide where Dan and I entered it. We really didn't know what was downstream, so we just shoved off. Just below the rushing traffic of the interstate I could see the current pick up speed and tumble over an old broken dam. It didn't look like a very big drop, at most what I'd call a class II rapid, but looking downstream I was strangely apprehensive. The spot looked familiar, and as we approached the rapid, I realized that on river left, just above where the interstate continued south on a sharp ridge, was where I had lived for the five months I'd survived with Margaret in Eugene. The memory did crazy things to my confidence. "That's where we lived while I was here," I shouted back at Dan, pointing from my bow seat toward the spot. "Just this side of that ridge, between the rock ridge and the interstate."

The water looked roughest to river left so I advised that we should go right, through a much calmer shoot and into a large eddy. From there we could have a straight path through the largest of the standing waves and on under the interstate bridge and past the bridge abutments. I was the one with more experience, so we took the route I proposed, a long sweeping arch of fast current, then lined up and headed down through a long series of stiff standing waves. The waves began breaking over the bow. At the bottom we were completely filled with water and slowly tipped over. The river was cold, and we didn't have on our lifejackets. I looked back and Dan was swimming with the submerged canoe.

I knew the real danger was wrapping Dan's brand new canoe around the bridge abutment, so I tugged and swam in the cold water to clear the boat before it broached on the round concrete abutment. We barely cleared the abutment; the water sloshed past so close we could hear it.

Then we were safe, the only real damage to our canoeing egos. Below the bridge the river was flat and cold. We swam the swamped canoe to the shallows and recovered there. As I stood in the shadow of the interstate bridge, I thought how I'd been toppled in a similar way twenty-five years before.

Why had this marriage lasted so much longer? You could say that it's love, but I loved Margaret, no matter how faulted that love grew to be when we were together. Betsy and I were so much older when we met. Maybe that's part of it—there was so much more water already over our dams. We rallied our passion around common goals—the writers project, building a house, making a place for us all.

When I came back from Eugene, I wandered around our house for days touching things to make sure they were still there—the table in the dining room, the couch, a piece of pottery, the railing on the back deck, the ears of both our hounds, my wife's back as she slept in the bed beside me. I've never had any doubt the world exists. Whether it could be counted on to stay, that's another story. We are never entirely settled. Time conspires against such certainty. If we're smart we count instead on the persistence of both perception and memory.

> The life in us is like the water in the river. It may rise
> this year higher than man has ever known it, and flood
> the parched uplands; even this may be the eventful
> year, which will drown out all our muskrats. It was not
> always dry land where we dwell.
>
> HENRY DAVID THOREAU, *Walden*

Flood

Our first December in the house the air was so warm it felt more like spring had somehow slipped the latch and walked in before winter even got started. It was unsettling. A front had moved in from the gulf, and warm rain fell ceaselessly. The creek filled up like Noah's flood.

Out back I could see the clay-colored water of the creek claiming Tommy's broad reach of bottomland through the trees. The flooded creek was four times as wide, the current pressing to the inside of the big sweeping bend behind our house. After a full day of rain, I stood on our back deck in the dark and listened to the current sloshing over dry winter grass along our lower trail, which was high and dry most of the year. The storm had parked on top of us.

Next day the warm rain finally stopped in the afternoon. When Rob came home from school at 4 o'clock, he was manic with excitement. He'd heard the creek first from the driveway and then caught a glimpse of it from the wide windows in the kitchen. He walked out on the deck and saw the creek flooding out of its banks, saw it was visiting our back yard.

"We've got to paddle," he said. Without thinking, I agreed, and we grabbed Russell, got our gear and boats out of the basement, and headed down to Glendale Shoals. We only had an hour and a half before we lost the light: just enough time for the lower section of Lawson's Fork if—famous last words— everything went according to our plan. We called from the cell phone and left a message for Betsy—meet us at the Goldmine Road Bridge at 5:30. Then we parked my truck below the Glendale dam. I glanced down the hill. The creek was very high and mighty—a roiling red flush of current roaring past like a southbound train.

We geared up quickly. There wasn't a moment of light to lose. We locked the truck and dragged our boats—Russell's yellow Riot, Rob's blue Liquid Logic, my orange Piranha—into a patch of kudzu and a backwash of litter at the edge of the SPACE preserve's field.

The boys were focused on the creek brawling past. I gave them one last safety talk mostly about strainers (trees down across the stream), how we had to stay vigilant about these obstructions and talk to each other about the best ways around, how to lean into a log if you get sideways. I said we had to move fast but safely downstream, one by one, to keep the light.

We snapped our spray skirts into place and peeled out onto the muddy lake that would usually be dry land. When we reached the edge of what would most days be the calm channel the flow took each of us, like catching a ride on a watery conveyer belt.

I led the way, followed by Rob, then Russell. Usually there were rocks through this narrow hallway of creek below the lower shoals, but in a flood even the rocks disappear, swallowed by the current. Floods are always significant natural events and often pose problems for humans. Kayakers rate rapids I to VI according to difficulty, but floods are random events figured in terms of probability—a yearly flood, a ten-year flood, a hundred-year flood. A "flood of record" in a ten-year period suggests that sometime during the next ten years a similarly sized flood will occur.

People die in rising water, and sometimes it's people like the three of us who have simply suffered a failure of judgment. That day we put on Lawson's Fork my worst failure of judgment was leaving too late. But I knew we could beat that if nothing unforeseen happened.

Every true kayaker knows what's best, but most will also ignore it at some point when the river calls. When things go wrong it's probably for two reasons—a group of paddlers puts in too late in the day, like we did, and they're overcome by darkness, or downstream obstacles wait in the wild riverbed to challenge their skill to survive, or sometimes, as was our case in December, both.

I had my doubts about going on the creek when Rob came home. After all, I was close to fifty years old. Rob is persuasive though, and I had promised him we'd do this together, fellow paddlers on a wild ride.

The creek was one of the things we really shared as stepfather and stepson. When he said, "We've got to paddle today," he was calling in a familiar debt and also making a challenge of sorts. He was opening up a room we could enter together, no matter how risky. I didn't know much about being a father, that the bulk of it is often about collapsing the rickety structures of what passes for teenage logic into short-lived disappointment.

Betsy wasn't home to extract me from my hasty commitment, to cast a shadow on this cockeyed plan to paddle a flooded December creek near sunset. They talk about "clouded judgment" as if life is blue summer sky invaded by storm. But judgment—and the lack of it—is something built up over time. There's usually little clarity, especially if nothing bad has ever really happened to you. It's more like the probability used in predicting flood events than it is some fixed rating system. I'd had lots of experiences at all water levels with Lawson's Fork, and all of them had been good. I felt I knew it well, and I thought I knew the dangers we were likely to face—cold water, fast current, a few rapids we could scout from the bank, and avoidable trees down in the current.

Rob and I had paddled the creek one other time in flood. It had peaked several years before at about 7 or 8 o'clock on a late May evening. I drove back and forth to Glendale to see the high water. The next day it was like a movie premiere on the bridge. People watched the power of the stream. The bridge shook with the volume going under it, and once while I was standing there, an entire cottonwood, leaves and all, sprawled over the dam and disappeared in the shoals below, resurfacing only once.

By noon the level had dropped, but the creek was still out of its banks. There was two feet of water coming over Glendale dam. We thought about putting in right behind our house, but I showed good judgment, concerned we would not be able to get off the creek before plunging over the dam.

Early that afternoon we drove to a local outfitter to rent Rob a creek boat for the paddle. He wasn't happy with the play boat he'd bought the summer before at camp. He wanted something with a little more volume for his first "flood run." I'd never seen Rob so talkative. He babbled on the whole way to the store about kayaking, paddle design, rodeo technique. He could sense that this was to be an epic run in his short history of paddling. In less than a half-hour we talked more than we had in the six years since Betsy and I had started dating.

Our first flood run down the creek we put in below the lower shoals at Glendale. Betsy dropped us off, and you could see the concern on her face. After all, a creek in flood is something to be respected. We told her not to worry and to meet us an hour later at the Goldmine Road bridge.

What current! It seemed to be moving thirty miles per hour, and when we put on we were quickly gone—downstream. The stretch just past the put-in was a fast flush of waves and curlers. We passed Betsy on the bank and shot on down. Later she told me that Rob looked relaxed as he fired past in his blue kayak, but I was gripping my paddle a little too hard, and my face showed a fear that to her didn't look healthy. It took us about thirty minutes to reach the Old Thompson Road bridge. Oil Can Rapid and Compound Rapid were completely washed out. The only real hazards—as we already knew—were the trees in the water. It was like paddling class III white water the whole way just avoiding the limbs and trunks. There were two or three ferries in front of strainers that were tough—especially on several sharp bends. The best thing about paddling a flood is the water level (we figured it was about seven feet above normal level), so we floated right over the top of all the logjams.

Little Five Falls—the quarter-mile shoals above Goldmine Road—was raging when we got there. We scouted the whole first rapid—the one we call You Otter Go Right because we saw an otter there once—and decided that the only way to run it safely was contrary to the name's directions, hugging the left shore. There was a tongue of water and then a huge standing wave where the river dropped over a big ledge.

After getting out to scout the situation I followed Rob down. I saw him disappear in front of me in the wave, and when I came through it I saw why—it was a six-foot standing wave, and it flipped me. When I Eskimo rolled to right myself, I was sitting in an eddy below the big wave. Rob was right beside me. When I popped back up he was laughing. "I did the same thing!" he said.

We floated on down through fast water to the next rapid and scouted what was left. There were huge hydraulics on river right and center all the way down, so Rob decided to run, hugging the left bank. I was rattled a little by the power of the first wave so I decided I would set a safety rope below for Rob and then put my boat on my shoulder and walk down past the worst of it. From there it was all fast water to the bridge. Betsy was waiting, a little worried since we were fifteen minutes late.

The December paddle with Rob and Russell started out badly. We pulled into an eddy below the first quarter mile of fast water, and I looked down and realized I'd set out on this epic paddle without my lifejacket. I'd forgotten to put it on in the rush to get on the water, and it was still back in the truck. I've been kayaking for over twenty years and never done anything that stupid. I was embarrassed and rattled. The light was slipping away, and it was my fault.

Showing what would later look clearly like a second sign of weak judgment, I decided to bushwhack through the woods, hit the road, go back a half-mile and retrieve my PFD in spite of the time. When I finally reached the road I ran into Ben Correll, a friend coming home from work, and he gave me a ride back up to the truck. "You've got to be crazy," Ben said after he listened to what we had in mind. After pleading with me to call it off, he dropped me back where I'd exited the woods to rejoin the boys. He drove off shaking his head.

We had a beautiful fast paddle to the big shoals. We followed each other down the creek, calling out routes around fallen trees, a tag-team descent of the flooded stream. We ran the first rapid again at the big shoals, the one where both Rob and I had flipped the year before. After we were safely through the first big wave I portaged the remainder of the rapids, setting rope, and the boys ran the rest. Their runs were damn perfect. They were careful in the long shoals, scouting every drop, watching out for each other, dodging trees and limbs as they worked their way down. I joined them back in the river at the bottom of the shoals and it's there that I dropped my guard. Darkness caught us, but I figured it would be fine. We were through the worst of it. I leaned back in my kayak and floated with the current.

About a quarter of a mile before the bridge where Betsy was waiting to pick us up, I came around a big sharp bend, and forty yards downstream a huge white oak formed a strainer from one bank to the other. I couldn't see any way around it. The creek had narrowed upstream in the small gorge at Little Five Falls, and in the bend it still had serious gradient and current. There were no eddies in the deep trough the creek had cut. The water was moving fast, straight for the trunk. I was leading the three of us right into the strainer, and I was helpless. I remember thinking, "You have five seconds to decide where you're going to hit this thing, and where you hit it is where the boys will hit it as well."

The oak was almost submerged on the river left; the root ball rested against the bank on river right and water was piling up against it. I split the difference and headed for a spot in the middle where it looked like if I hit it with enough speed I could jump over the wet crescent of exposed trunk. When I did hit I slid sideways and quickly disappeared under the log. It was one of those "oh shit, everything is slowing down and this is real bad" moments. I rolled under the log and scraped my way forward through limbs and brush. I didn't think I was going to come free. I opened my eyes but all I could see was the muddy water rushing past. My paddle was pulled out of my hands by the force of the water. Then somehow I flushed out the other side, and I was actually airborne for a moment, squirted out by the pressure of the water passing under the log. I felt like I'd been sucked through a portal into another world, another life.

I was turned completely around, without my paddle, like some wild white water rodeo move, and I somehow hit the water upright, just in time to see Russell flip upstream of the log as well. I couldn't see his face. It was worse than not seeing it, watching him disappear as I had under the log.

Without my paddle I had no real control of my boat in the fast current, so I quickly washed back into another strainer just downstream from the first, but in a little calmer water on the inside of the bend. There was still enough current to lodge me in a tangle of limbs, though. I was stuck in a tree in the middle of a flooded creek, but I wasn't in any danger of drowning. My head was above water, and I was still in my boat.

Once I recovered my senses a little all I could think about was the boys. I'd seen Russell but not Rob hit the tree and flip. Three or four minutes must have passed as I struggled with the tree, secured my own safety and tried to take stock of the situation, terrible minutes when I didn't know what I'd do, how to extract myself from the tree and current, and begin the search for the two missing boys.

My worst fear was that they were both still under the log. That's all I could think about for several moments. The week before I'd read Peter Heller's book *Come Hell or High Water,* about the Sangpo Gorge expedition in Tibet, and one passage from the book had been on my mind: "One moment the water tumbles around a bend, raucous with waves, pillowing around rocks, lapping and ripping the shore, and paddlers descend in bright boats," he'd written. "The next moment a boat is up-side down, pressed into a sieve of a downed tree or undercut rock, the hull piling the current, gleaming in the sun. You retrieve the body, however long that takes, and you stand in shock on the shore, and the river flows just as it did. The rush and sift and gurgle. The rapid looks the same; it is innocent, as beautiful as moving water always seems. What is cleaved is your own heart, and the past from that moment, and the sense that you can ever relive anything."

Now I was in such a moment. I feared the worst. What would be "cleaved" would be my own heart. From where I sat, tangled in the branches of a topped tree troubled by surging current, it didn't look like it could go any other way.

Then I heard a voice call from high and dry on the bank. "John!" I looked over and there stood Russell, fifteen yards across the current. I took me a moment to realize what I was seeing. It seemed so impossible. How had Russell gone from under the log to standing on the bank? I'd have to wait a while to get the answer.

"Where's Rob?" I finally yelled over the sound of the flooded creek. I couldn't hear his answer. He yelled something, but I couldn't hear over the roar of the water. That's when I pushed out of my boat, letting it go like a shed skin, and it headed downstream. For a moment it was more frightening being in the tree out of my boat. Without the protection and buoyancy of the boat it was simply me and the tree, and I was still tangled in the branches. I clung to it for a moment then let go.

I swam like hell to cross the fifteen yards of the flooded creek and made the eddy behind the big muddy root ball of the log where Russell was standing. I was still in water over my head. The normal creek bottom was somewhere below me under fifteen feet of muddy water.

Russell's boat and my blue paddle circled next to me in the muddy eddy. I quickly grabbed boat and paddle and hauled the gear up the bank. It wasn't until I had dragged myself out of the water that I looked up and saw that Rob was just downstream of me, scrambling up out of the creek himself, holding on to his boat and paddle.

We did a quick gear check. My boat was long gone, and Russell had lost his paddle. Rob had all his gear—boat, paddle. The three of us squeezed together in a clumsy hug, and then we huddled for a minute. The boys said they had each hit the log exactly where I did and flushed under just like me. Russell said the most frightening thing to him was seeing my face as I went under on the upstream side of the log. He said he could hear me say, "Shit!" Rob described being caught in the branches under the log for a moment and pushing out and strangely simply bobbing up in the eddy.

"Don't tell Betsy what happened," I said, conspiring, as men will sometimes do to keep the worst news from the women. We sent Rob out ahead to work his way along the bank through the woods to the bridge where Betsy was waiting. If she saw my orange boat pass by we'd decided Rob would tell her I'd dropped my boat portaging a rapid.

Rob disappeared ahead of us into the dark December woods. I helped Russell with his boat, and we made our way toward the bridge where his mother and my wife waited. When we came out of the woods the look on Betsy's face was somewhere between relief and fear, but it quickly softened into relief. We told her the real story as we all four stood together on the bridge. Betsy listened, but all she really wanted was to get us home safely.

As we loaded gear she told her side of the story: when she'd seen my orange boat rush past empty and upside down, riding the muddy current, she'd run up the hill to a house because her cell phone didn't work at the bridge. She'd found someone home and called Ben Correll. He'd told her the story about picking me up on Emma Cudd Road earlier.

"Call Fred Parrish," Betsy had told him. "Call whoever you need." No one came for fifteen minutes, and she stood on the bridge not knowing what had happened to us before Rob finally appeared from the woods with his story to calm her.

Betsy loaded Russell and me into the car to retrieve my truck. Rob stayed with what was left of the gear. Up Goldmine Road Betsy was finally able to get back in cell phone range, and a quick call headed off a full lifesaving effort, though Ben and Fred were close to calling in the professionals.

I learned to love rivers thirty years ago, long before I fell in love with Betsy and her boys. It would have been impossible back then for me to imagine that loving rivers could lead to the near tragedy of that day on the creek, to losing Rob and Russell, to how close I came to leaving Betsy without one, two, or all three of us, standing alone on a bridge in the falling darkness as her husband's orange kayak floated past upside down in the last light.

We circled back home that evening. Russell rode with Betsy, and Rob rode in the truck with me and the two surviving boats. It was still unseasonably warm for December, even well after dark. We were wet, dressed in the clothes we'd paddled in. We were mostly quiet, but getting closer to home I finally broke the silence and asked Rob how he felt when saw me hit the log, then Russell. Was he afraid when he saw us disappear one after another, then felt himself get sucked under as well?

"I wasn't scared for long," he said with what passes for reflection in a teenage boy. Then he got a little more serious. "I've been paddling for three years and nothing bad has ever happened to me. What happened to us today was a good thing in some ways. I think it made us all better paddlers."

"I don't know how good it was," I said. "I think we almost died."

"You know, John, I couldn't believe you went," Rob said after pausing for a moment. He smiled. "That's the most spontaneous thing I've ever seen you do since I've known you. I think it was good for you."

As Rob talked I remembered the first time we'd paddled Lawson's Fork as a group—mother, boyfriend, two young boys. Betsy and I were still years away from the commitment of marriage, but she'd fallen in love with Lawson's Fork at the same time she'd fallen in love with me. We'd bought four kayaks so we could all "explore the interior" as she liked to call it when we'd drag the two young boys off to paddle poky piedmont streams.

We'd put in on the same section of creek for a first family descent of a stream with a little white water. The creek was full, but nothing Betsy and the boys couldn't handle. The rapids in Little Five Falls would be class II or III at best, and we'd work our way down slowly. Rob was maybe thirteen and Russell was ten or eleven, but they'd both already paddled mountain white water at the camp where they went in the summers. Our four new Perception Acadias, recreational kayaks more suited to lake paddling than white water, weren't even scratched up yet. Rob already wanted more—more white water, a better boat, more adrenaline.

Russell, still a little apprehensive, stayed back with us, no matter how badly he wanted to bolt out front, but Rob paddled thirty yards ahead the whole day. When we reached Little Five Falls it freaked me out a little chasing Rob down each ledge. I had lost control of the trip, and a thirteen-year-old was now leading us down through the rapids. We even ended up naming one drop with a nice hole at the bottom "Rob's Dip" because from the eddy we sat in upstream all we saw was Rob completely disappear in the hole before he bobbed out the other side upright. To this day that's what we call the spot. I realized that day watching Rob paddle sullenly out in front of us that marriage is a flood, and family is probably the one-hundred-year flood in anybody's life. I looked over at Rob the day we nearly died and realized all I really know about him is what I'd seen in a dozen photo albums under the window. Their early lives as infants and children is uncharted water for me, and now I've been pitched into it midstream.

When we arrived home Rob went straight for a shower. The two boats and all the gear stayed in the truck. I'd worry about it all in the morning. I'd think about my lost boat then as well, whether it was worth mounting a recovery expedition to find it. I figured it was probably long gone from Lawson's Fork, in a tree somewhere downstream on the Pacolet River, out of place, beaten up by riding the cresting, clay-colored flood a mile or two. Gear was the last thing on my mind when we arrived home after our ordeal.

I was more than a little spooked by nearly dying, and I didn't really know what to do to shake it. Russell and Betsy had beaten us back by five minutes, and when I slipped inside the side door I could see Betsy was already settled into her reading chair in the living room. I don't remember what she said. We talked for awhile, and I told her I'd be back in a minute, that I wanted to take the dogs down by the creek. Toby and Ellie Mae jumped at the chance to head out for an evening bonus walk.

It was still way too warm for December. I was in shorts from paddling. The three of us descended the hill through the dormant wildflowers. I could hear the creek making that freight train sound, still out of its banks. We walked to the edge of the floodwaters where the creek reached the path at the bottom of our yard. I couldn't see far out on the moving current, but I could feel that it was cooler close to the water. I thought how the water passing me would be five miles downstream and under the log that nearly killed us in less than an hour. Then I thought how long the night would have been for the search and rescue crew had we not made it out of the creek.

Both dogs sniffed at the edge of the muddy lapping water, looked around, and seemed content to head back up the hill. I looked up toward the house, and the windows in the back wall were all lit up. With the lights on, the house looked like a big clipper ship intent on floating out onto the dark, marauding creek. The dogs looked too, wondering why I'd paused. It was time to go in, they announced with their impatience.

Settling down doesn't have to include trials like we had that December day. It's possible to know a landscape and love it without coming close to death. I've never thought of myself as one of those extreme adventure types. Now, when the creek floods I hear a different sound than that December afternoon, and I remember, and I hope I never come that close to losing all this again.

Foolish me,
To think my wine
Would never turn.

JIM HARRISON AND
TED KOOSER,
Braided Creek

Alamos

Back in my thirties and early forties I hunted for love by gathering freedom, excitement, and adventure, and I often found them by traveling away from my hometown. I completed long hikes on the Appalachian Trail, in the Cascades of Oregon, and along the Pacific Coast in Washington. One summer I carried a pack twenty miles into the Wind River Range of Wyoming. I camped there with Terry Ferguson, his brother, and their friends in the Cirque of the Towers, turned around ten days later, and hiked out.

Whatever I was looking for back then I found "out there" among mountains and rivers and deserts and not in a suburban house or a city apartment. The instruments of my quest were a one-man tent, a sleeping bag, a water-purification pump, a journal, and enough rations for whatever duration faced me on the road or the trail.

Looking back I realize I was as dehydrated as the dried food I carried, and the reason I moved so much was that I had to in order to stay moist. Moisture for me was motion. It was what kept me alive. If I wasn't moving, I was planning to move, signing up for whatever "adventure travel" was offered. In twenty years I wore out three sets of boots. I stayed fit and ready.

Once I walked from the Irish Sea to the North Sea along the route of Hadrian's Wall with three college colleagues. Another summer I hiked 150 miles of Offa's Dyke in Wales, tramping the route of Wordsworth's pilgrimage up the Wye River to the ruins of Tintern Abbey and then climbing high into the Black Mountains along Cat's Back Ridge, a steep razor scarp with spectacular drop-offs on either side.

I didn't know it at the time, but these hikes were some of my last pilgrimages into whatever wild I was pursuing. Already I'd turned some corner in my soul—choosing to walk between bed-and-breakfasts where we could settle for the evening and swill local ale at the pub rather than haul camping gear down the trail.

That summer hiking Hadrian's Wall we followed the ruins of the great barrier built to keep wildness out of an empire. The Romans liked order. They quarried rock, dug trenches, erected berms, cleared forest to keep the outer edge of their empire tidy. The hike became a metaphor for my life transition—exploring the marginal country between a coming settlement and diminished wildness.

Often along the way we gained enough altitude to see far off across the English countryside. I was always surprised. It was beautiful and inviting, but what I remember was how tame the distances seemed—rolling pastures, stone walls, cottages, small stands of trees, roads proceeding along hillsides and disappearing behind a curve only to reappear further on, and the clouds standing above it all like anvils. The English had subdued their land with settlement centuries before but had somehow maintained more rural lands than much of America's settled East, where I was from.

There was nothing held hostage in the view, no wildness ready to break out from ragged corners of the picture, as happens in America's West. All the corners in England had been tucked and smoothed by grazing centuries before. Even the South Carolina countryside seemed wild compared to the pastoral north country of England with Hadrian's Wall cutting across it. Maybe it's the trees in South Carolina, and here you can disappear around a bend and be swallowed not by geometric fields but by acres of a ragged grove.

Settlement in America expands outward from tiny points of habitation—a village becomes a town, which becomes a city. Culture has created a geometric landscape—square lots and square houses add up to squared-off subdivisions. There's a headlong tumble to it. In England settlement covered the land long ago like a mood, a fever you can catch, and British law still allows for public access to private property—the "right to roam"—hence its vast National Trail System.

Sometimes, while walking Hadrian's Wall, I pretended that I was not in England but America, maybe four hundred years in the future. If we were to ever really settle America, this type of "countryside" is what I hope we'll evolve into—pastures, fields, and villages, a trail system winding through, not a vast system of supersuburbs connected by four-lane highways.

Back then, if I wasn't walking, I was driving country roads, leaving the interstates behind. The summer of 1992 I put fourteen thousand miles on my gray Mazda truck, coast to coast, and not one mile of it on a four-lane. In late May, after school was out, I left Spartanburg, crawling like a snake just out of hibernation through North Carolina, Tennessee, Virginia, West Virginia, Kentucky, and Ohio before I crossed Kentucky again, and then the Mississippi. I had my black kayak and blue mountain bike secured to the roof rack and a plywood bed built in the pickup's topper with a single futon for a mattress. I'd stored my camping gear under the bed—sleeping bag, one-man backpacking tent, camp stove—and stashed enough emergency peanut butter, water, and beans and rice for a month. I was as self-contained as the space shuttle.

In North Carolina I stopped to paddle several times—the French Broad, the Nantahala, familiar rivers, like spending the night with cousins, and then pushed further north and west. I wanted to get out of my comfort zone. Every mile by myself I felt more at home in my truck.

I spent most of July in Wyoming and Montana. Early August I drove to Oregon. Coming through the mountains east of Eugene I dropped slowly down into a tiny town's central square at midnight. A full moon shone as I crawled through switchback turns. Mule deer drifted in front of the truck all the way from the pass. Coyotes howled from the ridges that night as I slept in the back of my truck outside a closed café.

I stayed a week on the Northern Umpqua River and paddled every day. The water was clear, and the waves broke on the bow of my black Dagger Response like ice as I surfed in rapids. My friends who ran the outfitter's service were newly married, and they quarreled every night, about what I wasn't sure. Their truce held during the day, but in the evening I could hear their raised voices in their cabin for hours before silence finally filled the valley, and we all could sleep. On the day I left they told me I should visit a fire lookout on a nearby peak, as if they wanted to show me a role model for real solitude. It was a six-mile hike in, but the fellow who manned it liked visitors. When I arrived he was sitting high in the lookout drinking herbal tea. We talked about Jack Kerouac, Gary Snyder, and Lew Welch, literary lookouts who had served as fire spotters in Cascade towers. He showed me pictures of a helicopter that had crashed delivering supplies years before and a twisted metal piece of it he'd kept as a souvenir. I signed his guest book and walked back to the trailhead by dusk.

Mid-August I headed south to meet a group of field-biology

friends in the northwestern Mexican state of Sonora, where they were catching Mexican beaded lizards, a big poisonous reptile that's a cousin to the Gila monster. There I fell hard for a young Spanish professor along on the trip. She was dark and romantic. She had traveled with the Contras in Central America and hitched all over Spain and North Africa. We camped together outside Alamos, a colonial silver-mining town. Each night we rode the roads with the scientists and collected snakes and lizards; then, after dark, they walked up long desert ridges to explore the abandoned silver mines where they camped out and, at dawn, set up mist nets at the mine entrances to catch bats returning from foraging.

I liked riding the roads but avoided the trips to the dark mines, instead listening in the mornings as the explorers returned from the bat caves with stories of millions of Mexican free-tailed bats clinging to the rock vaults above them. I don't know what I was avoiding. I regret not following, not descending into the Mexican hillsides. I stayed on the surface, often went into town, sat on a bar's shaded verandah, drank beer, and sketched the colonial arches of the zocalo and the Alamos cathedral in my journal.

The Spanish professor, another twenty-eight-year-old, proved elusive all week, though finally when everyone else left the campground in Alamos and headed north, she asked if I wanted to follow her rattle-trap old blue Toyota into the Mexican backcountry to look for a magic canyon. For two days we were truly off-road, off-book, and on our own. We broke down several times, ended up hopelessly lost, and survived on peanut M&Ms, green Mexican oranges, and water pumped and filtered from rare local streams. She led me deep into Mexico on cow paths toward the canyon she'd only heard rumors about.

We dead-ended once at a flash-flooding river, and another time the road simply disappeared in a dry canyon we had to back down. After a day of driving we slept in the back of the truck, curled affectionately in each other's arms. She talked in her sleep in Spanish, and I would wake and listen, trying to make out the foreign phrases. Coyotes lived in the dry yellow hills, and they yapped all night.

The next day we finally found the canyon. A small bold stream tumbled from the narrow entrance. Approaching, I was stung by a wasp and had a bad allergic reaction, so I did not hike in. She waited an hour to make sure I didn't die from the shock, then left me sitting there, off on her own adventure. I watched as she disappeared into the canyon.

That wasp sting stopped me cold. It was like an antivenom for my wandering. I'd never had such a reaction before. It worried me deeply that something so small could cause such a quick and decisive change. I sat in the shade all day and thought a great deal about the edges of my own wildness. All the metaphors I was living were quite clear—"off-road," "four-wheeling," "off the grid," "in the weeds." They all occurred to me during my long day of waiting for my new romantic interest to return.

How long could I live like this? I was thirty-eight, ten years past the period most people settle in our culture. What was I doing in Mexico chasing a younger woman, waiting in the shadow of the entrance to a dark canyon for her return? That summer I'd already driven over ten thousand miles. I'd paddled wild rivers, climbed to the top of a Cascade peak, gazed out of a fire lookout at miles of trees, fallen in love.

The professor brought me a gift when she returned hours later—two small pottery shards with a ghost of red pigment. She'd found them near a spring in the canyon, a token of long-ago settlement. She said the spot, a little paradise, was tucked back in the canyon wall, hidden from view. She'd had to follow the spring run up into the cliffs from where it refreshed the main creek. She was sorry I'd never see it. She had sat there for a few minutes in the shade of the rocks, and it was then she'd seen the fragments of an ancient pot in the dust at her feet.

On my way back across the country I drove alone on back roads. I ate in mom-and-pop cafés, what William Least Heat Moon called "two-calendar joints" along his "blue highways." I stopped at Mammoth Cave National Park in Kentucky, bought a ticket and finally went deep into a cave. They turned the lights out when we were all in. We stood there in a darkness I'd never felt before. I was lonely and tired from all my travel. There weren't even any bats for company.

The next day I crawled back to Spartanburg in my truck, spent to the core. The professor and I made a go of it for a year or so, and then she went off to the Peace Corps in Yemen and, after that, moved for good to Arizona. It took me two or three more relationships with younger women before I finally settled down with Betsy, someone near my own age. I can't imagine a summer on the road now, though for years I couldn't imagine anything else.

We must begin by remembering beyond history.

PAUL SHEPARD, *Coming Home to the Pleistocene*

Our Indian Country

After we moved in I began thinking about ways to set up a series of walks to settle me, a different one every day. I scoured the maps for trails and cut-through streets. I sketched in my head a set of pilgrim paths. What better way to get the lay of my land, to get acquainted with my own walkable country, to find what John Hanson Mitchell calls in *Ceremonial Time* "the great undiscovered country of the nearby"?

In the end though, because of time and laziness, it all came down to one daily half-mile evening walk, always in the same direction, out and back. Every evening at about 5:30 Betsy and I take our daily ritual walk. We leave our house on Tempo Court and stroll west with the dogs down Mustang Drive. At the bottom of the hill we turn southwest onto Starline Drive and enter Pierce Acres proper.

Even on warm February days Betsy dresses for the cold in a wool sweater and down vest and a cap, though it's often only in the midforties. She hates winter and jokes, "Global warming is my friend."

I remind her the climate here hasn't always been so balmy. Twelve thousand years ago when the first humans probably wandered up our creek the weather was still under the influence of Wisconsin glaciations—and an ice sheet a mile high loomed only three hundred miles north. There were big game hunters then—the Clovis people—migrating through what is now our backyard. They might have used fire to drive mammoths, mastodon, and bison roaming the future suburbs of Spartanburg, and their culture was based upon such hunts, not shopping at Wal-Mart. Local artifact hunters have found Clovis points and stone tools here in Spartanburg County, so we know they were present.

"You need to dress for the cold only six months a year," I say. "Back then it was much colder." Betsy shivers just thinking about it. "South of that cold wall of ice were grass lands, pine forests and spruce."

By eight or ten thousand years ago native people were wandering long trails up from the coast. They camped seasonally on these very ridges around our house. The artifacts we've found prove it so. When Pleistocene glaciations came to an end the climate and flora changed, and the piedmont landscape that developed after the ice retreated north was much like what you might see now in the woods of Canada, seven hundred miles north—northern conifers like hemlock, and hardwoods—beech, elm, and birch. Then as the climate warmed even more, oak, hickory, and sweet gum moved in. By the time that happened this would have been a landscape we would recognize as our own.

I can recite archaeology's story of the human settlement of the area around our house in order of occupation—Paleo-Indian (before 8000 B.C.), Archaic (8000–1000 B.C.), Woodland (1000 B.C.–A.D. 1600), Historic (after A.D. 1600). This is a story I've come to live by. It's one of the base templates for my dreaming, and in it about eight thousand years ago, the Archaic period hunters and gatherers began to exploit all the local resources—fish, shellfish, squirrels, waterfowl, turtles, as well as acorns, walnuts, seeds, and roots. These bands of hunters and gatherers moved great distances up and down the rivers and spent seasons in different areas. They "wintered" along the coastal rivers or on the coast itself; there are vast shell middens that speak to their appetite for oysters.

In springtime they moved upstream to higher ground to hunt deer, and when the weather turned cooler they traced the rivers back to coastal camps. It is from this period that archaeologists also found the first evidence of trading. The South Carolina piedmont region had a prominent soapstone industry beginning over four thousand years ago. The bowls "mined" here from the exposed outcroppings were transported all over the Southeast. "The earliest Crock-Pots" are what Terry Ferguson calls the soft gray stone bowls of these early people.

I like to think of the Archaic period as one of the most successful stretches of human history—seasonal migrations up and down rivers hunting deer and turkey, gathering fruit and nuts, harvesting freshwater mussels along the waterways. This way of life developed then continued unchanged for thousands of years. "They hunted and gathered in this very creek bottom, lived and died here," I explain to anyone who will listen, maybe sounding a little too much like *The Clan of the Cave Bears.*

Betsy's always a good audience as I revel in the deep past. On our walks she never asks for hard evidence; she only needs the excitement in my voice to please her. I have a tendency to romanticize the lives of these early hunters and gatherers, to make them into our own ecofriendly versions of Adam and Eve. They shared so much with us, same size brains, core spiritual practices, burial of their dead, and a love for the same wild meats many of my neighbors still hunt along the creek. How to get back to their world if not through such projection?

I can't seem to stop imagining how it must have been when those wandering bands stopped circling through the woods on their seasonal journeys through the piedmont. The little evidence we have gives my imagination enough to go on. Paleo-Indian period hunters disappeared when the bison and mastodons were gone, and then thousands of years later, the Archaic period hunters and gatherers stopped just wandering through on their annual walks up from the coast, settling instead into more permanent village life. These migratory people covered the same trails for over ten thousand years—five hundred generations walking up the Broad River, same creeks and rivers every year, same camp sites, same game and flowering plants blooming and fruiting at the same time each season in the same fields, give or take a week or two.

Our landscape's so altered now that the Archaic period hunters who knew it so intimately (for intimacy is a function of time) would most likely not even recognize it. Where are the old-growth groves they knew? Where are the plants they picked and boiled in their soapstone bowls stashed year-to-year in familiar campsites? How did they react when the shad ran up from the coast? Novelist W. G. Sebald says in *The Rings of Saturn* that history demands a lie—"a falsification of perspective"—because we are the survivors. "We see everything from above, see everything at once, and still we do not know how it was."

On our walks we've discovered our Indian country, strong and steady for the full thirty minutes we're out the door. As we stroll we contemplate our neighbors, their yards, and what they say about how they live, the vast floodplain stretching north, south, east, and west. I push my mind back into the past, stretching my notions of time. I watch the dogs at the ends of their leashes and try to imagine the world they smell, what their feet tell them about the place, if their eyes see anything different than we do. Our dogs are like living Geiger counters tethered to our arms, registering the momentary pulsations of wildness out there beyond their noses. As I walk, listen, and explore, the world is radioactive with wildness. I glow with it when I return home, and it spills out here onto the page.

Not everyone sees time as something deep, something you can send a shaft into and prowl like a miner. To most of our suburban friends and neighbors time is a crust of days, weeks, years, maybe generations at the most. There are probably even a few in the houses we pass who are biblically inclined, who believe this vast and mysterious universe was created at 9 a.m. on October 23, 4004 B.C. "Time is not on our side," my friend Deno says when I begin to wax poetically about deep time. "You're lucky. Time's something most of us fight against to get through the day. It's not often something that nurtures us—instead it whittles us away."

Our dogs always urge us on. We're not on these daily walks for history, they always remind us. Ellie and Toby lead the way on our walks out and back into the neighborhood. We let them off the leashes the first few hundred yards. We're always headed away from the creek and its deep set of summoning scents. If we went in that direction the dogs might disappear for hours into the privet. Headed west, they trot happily along. Going down the hill on Mustang Drive we pass vacant parcels thick with trees, still forest, not yet "wooded lots." At the bottom of the hill we often pause and gaze into an empty lot, a finger of floodplain cut off from the rest by the fill dirt that forms Mustang Drive's entry into our neighborhood. A local church owns this low, wooded parcel, and there have been "for sale" signs on the two sides fronting on the roads since we moved in. A church elder who lives up on Starline says the church is anxious to sell. The lot was left to them in a parishioner's estate, and the cash would help pay off the note on their new education building.

We see him out working on our walks and tell him it looks to us like it would be better left "natural." He shakes his head. "It's a bargain. Somebody can timber it for profit and then fill it to build," he says. "It's a good location. Right now it's just a mosquito breeding ground."

It's the wetness that bothers him. A perennial spring bubbles up on the lot's low south end and drains toward the creek through a concrete culvert under Mustang Drive. Our neighbor calls this area a "swamp," but with a little attention it's easy to see it's not a swamp. Most of the lot is dry, though low. Swamps have trees in standing water; this tiny wet area is more a bog or a seep. There are grasses and sedges growing in the moist spots.

The water is red where the spring bubbles out of the ground and red all the way to the culvert. At first this red tint made the little seep look polluted, and we were paranoid that someone had buried barrels of chemicals here. When we pointed out the red run-off to a biologist friend on an afternoon walk, he laughed and outlined a much less astonishing conclusion than the fear we had located a Superfund site: the red seep on the corner is the natural product of an odd native bacteria, the *Gallionella* and *Leptothrix* species. This native fauna utilizes the heavy iron content of the soil, and their colonies form little clumps of iron ore. That's what makes the water run red. If there were enough of the colonies, ore nodules would form bog iron. "If there were more, you could mine bog iron like the Vikings once did," the biologist explained.

In March and April, a large stand of may-apple, a wildflower with one or two broad, nodding leaves shaped like open hands, tilts toward the south. When we're walking we can't miss the expanse of may-apple. It's quite startling the way the waxy white flowers emerge in a mass on the low boggy slope above the spring and cover the ground in a bright green colony. It's something we looked forward to every spring, though the plants are quite common in the piedmont if you know where to look. Native Americans used the root's extract as a purgative and to treat skin disease. Today the alkaloids found in them are used to treat leukemia. The leaves and seeds are poisonous if eaten, but the ripe fruits can be made into jelly. It's truly a plant of many uses. When we want to see each plant's single white flower we wade out into the colony and turn up a leaf. We've always liked this botanical secrecy, this lovely surprise kept from all but those who know where to look.

The spring could have been in use for thousands of years, maybe even since the first Paleo-Indian bands roamed these ridges now covered with subdivision houses. Springs often helped mark camping sites for early people, much as they do now on long-distance trails. They would have known where the springs rise and made use of them. A spring was special in the days before wells and city water. You could even say sacred.

What could be more sacred than running water? Along with fire, water has "occupied the fullest measure of man's religious thought" as one historian of Native American spirituality has put it. In many creation stories the world itself is born of water, and purification by water is often a part of ancient rites. Christ himself said if a man can't be born of water, he couldn't enter the kingdom. Does the church with title to this spring know they hold title to something holy? They fill their baptism font with tap water when all they'd have to do is drive out to this property and fill it from the living land.

Last March our neighbor spent three or four hours every Saturday cutting underbrush on the lot, piling it high, then working to train the spring's flow into a pipe so that the lot looked less boggy. He waved as we walked past. What debt does that church owe the spring? The creek? What do they owe to the deer and fox and raccoon and bobcat that have worn a steady path to the spring? How about the debt to the three or four mud turtles who live in the muck around the seep and return to it after they lay eggs? Or the salamanders who breed there, or spring peepers who congregate there in late February nights like this, singing their brains out for love?

It's a complex ecosystem we've bought into out here on the edge of the suburbs. One man's seep is another man's swamp. One woman's frogspawn is another woman's mosquito alley. One church's windfall is someone else's storehouse for diversity. We know the neighbor understands all this, because we've talked to him about it. In spite of our discussions, he still sees the lot as part of the neighborhood, a piece of real estate to be bought and sold, made level, built upon. We, in contrast, see it as connected to the wilder floodplain to its south. He sees it as what it can become—a home for some family, an entry on the tax rolls, the partial retirement of a church debt. We imagine it back into the wild fold—living spring, flowing water, and hardwood bottom moist all year. Paying for the education hall is a human problem. Keeping the spring running is what ecotheologian Thomas Berry would call "an earth problem," or a way to stop the devastation of the planet. Earth problems occupy much of our talk as we walk, and these little discussions we get into with our neighbors always seem so dramatic.

When the hunter-gatherers finally settled I don't think it was quite as dramatic as what we're going through here on the edge of Spartanburg. Over a period of a few thousand years the gathering of plants led to experiments with horticulture and eventually the beginnings of agriculture with corn traded up from Mesoamerica. By 1000 A.D. the Indians we now call "Woodland" were relying heavily on cultivated plants. This led to larger populations and a more settled way of life. They began hunting with bows and arrows instead of the atlatl whose point I had found on the hillside outside our house. Some people claim it's not that far a leap—through time or space—from the early villages of the Woodland period to our own suburbs. Once we humans began farming it wasn't really that far to the split-level and Home Depot.

Once I asked Terry Ferguson about hard evidence of these ancient cultures up and down the creek, and he prefaced everything he told me with "could be," "may be," and "that sounds plausible from what the scant archeological record shows." When Terry starts talking this way I pull out the hard evidence I keep in my pocket, one of the white quartz atlatl points we found on our hilltop, hold it up and ask Terry if it is real. "Precisely," he says. "It's only hard evidence like this point that tells the real story."

Then I lose my traction on the real and start speculating again, talking about how so-and-so says there's an Indian mound in a field just downstream. Terry acknowledges the point is authentic, a piece of the Archaic period weathered from the context of a piedmont hillside, but he scoffs at all this talk of mounds, reminds me how I've got to be careful with the past. There's no hard evidence of mound builders active on Lawson's Fork, though a Mississippian mound does rise out of a Broad River bottom only thirty miles east, in Lockhart, South Carolina. "That's private land down there too," he said. "The state's tried to buy it for preservation."

Most accounts of Indian culture in the Southeast during the historic period come to us from the journals of Spanish explorers. I'd love to place these wandering conquistadors in our backyard, but much to my disappointment, contemporary historical evidence has shown that in the spring of 1540 De Soto passed fifty miles east of where we've built our dream house, choosing to look for gold in the Catawba watershed rather than the Pacolet or the Broad. In the 1930s a stone was plowed up in a field north of here, and it's now called "Pardo's Stone." It is in the regional history museum. If authentic it's the oldest European artifact in South Carolina. On its surface among deep plow marks is a small arrow pointing north and an etched date, 1566, the year Juan Pardo walked inland from near what's today coastal Beaufort.

Did the Spanish explorer or someone from his party pass this way, possibly right along this ridge top and on up Lawson's Fork from the coast? I like to think so, though recent archeological evidence sets Pardo's route closer to De Soto's earlier one. So is there any chance of an undiscovered "Pardo's Stone" out there somewhere on our land? "Could be," Terry says. "Could be, but not likely."

Like De Soto or Pardo I search for gold, though for me it's more likely to come from an unexpected sunset on these evenings we walk the dogs. It's no thousand-mile journey I'm on, only a late afternoon stroll, and soon enough we always reach the corner of Fairlane and Lake Forest Drive, where out of habit we always turn around.

I like our short walk to the corner with the floodplain to our south. There I can forget about the realities of today and revel in the past, thinking myself forward through what I know of twelve thousand years of Native American history.

When I tell my friends that I'm writing now about our Indian country, most of them say, "Oh, the Cherokees." Some say the Cherokees are connected to this place, though if they were here they were late arrivals for the party, one of the last in a long line of native occupants before the Europeans showed up and settled in with their property rights and all the oddball ideas that led to suburban individualism.

After 1500 the Cherokees could have used this creek as hunting territory and as a buffer zone between themselves and their traditional enemies to the east, the Catawbas. They did not establish permanent towns on the rivers of Spartanburg County. The closest Cherokee permanent settlements, the "lower towns," were on the Keowee River, sixty miles southwest.

Native languages are often poetic, leaning hard up against the world, and they named everything—bodies of water, spots where something unusual happened, the sites of skirmishes and battles. There's no reason not to believe that this landscape around us wasn't once held together by a web of Indian words and stories the way Tom Pierce's Ford auto names now define the Pierce Acres subdivision. I could not reconstruct the sounds of the native languages spoken here. Native Americans will never haunt this landscape again with their original ancient lexicon. The map they carried of this place is forever vanished, impossible to recover.

Some moments I get a feeling they're still around. As Faulkner liked to say, the past is never really past. Almost ten years ago, on the final day of the weeklong Lawson's Fork festival, Betsy held a big gathering on the ball fields below Spartanburg High School. There were hundreds of people present that day, and we saw a huge red-tailed hawk land high on one of the light poles. The hawk sat as the gospel choir sang "The Water is Wide," and it stayed put while the Spartanburg Philharmonic played "The River" by Virgil Thompson.

It was only when the music was over and our invited Cherokee medicine man walked up to the podium that the hawk began to cry out. The medicine man wore a white western shirt, jeans, and cowboy boots. He had a big leather belt with a jade buckle. Against the strong April sun he wore a billed "Cherokee, N.C." ball cap. He blessed the four cardinal directions with an eagle feather and burning sage much as our friend Meg had done at our groundbreaking. He shook a rattle and offered up prayers to all the winged, hoofed, and footed beings in attendance, seen and unseen. As the crowd listened he explained how the land along this creek had been the land of his people for centuries. Then he began to tell a story about how the earth around us was made. It was a story I'd discovered reading anthropologist James Mooney many years before, how the animals had been present when the world was formed and it was all covered with water. I remember it as an early version of the flood story, with a vulture landing on a mud flat, and as she pulled her wings from the mire the Appalachian mountains and piedmont hills were pulled into relief. What impressed me about the story was the way the animals somehow predated the planet, how they were mythical creatures older than time.

The creek was praised and welcomed into our human community. The hawk seemed to listen while the animals were celebrated for their part in creation. As the medicine man began to address the audience the hawk's cries began to punctuate the ceremonies like applause. I took it as approval for the work we were doing and thought of that day as a coordinate on a map I was tracing of the creek.

Now, six years later, we map the place with our steps. The topography is abrupt where Starline Drive straightens out and heads southwest and parallels the creek. I'm sure the early Indians would have had a name for this spot—"Where the ridge falls away," or "There are no mosquitoes here." There are suburban houses on the high ridge along the north side of the road, and the vast deep floodplain broods to the south.

Like the Cherokees and all the people before them, what we want is intimacy, which only comes over time. It takes more than the mind or the nose to understand a place.

We round the curve on Starline; this part of the walk is a real no-man's-land and often a dumping ground since it's mostly hidden from the view of the neighbors. As we walk here we always see something new tossed on the side of the road or down the hill into the bottom—bags of ivy clippings, old shelving units, appliances, bed springs, rounds of pine. It's also the preferred deposit for white plastic sacks of illegal beer cans consumed by underage teens on Saturday night and the final resting place for the trimmings of this year's crape myrtle branches. The latter can decompose slowly; the former has to be picked up by someone at some point, often us.

As we walk along Starline Drive Betsy points out our modern day artifacts flung from a speeding car—numerous beer cans, cigarette packs, even a bank statement sodden and crumpled along the edge of our newfound wilderness. Are these beer cans our new arrowheads? "You shoot a shotgun and you don't pick up the pellets," a friend once said when I asked them why there were so many Indian artifacts. "Points were expendable." We don't send teenage boys out to walk the boundary lines of tribal territory anymore. Instead we buy them cars and hand them the keys. They throw beer cans out on an isolated road, and we think it's the end of the world. But worlds don't end so easily. I kick the cans to the asphalt and stomp them flat. I pick them up. They'll go in our recycling bin to be made into more cans that will end up on somebody else's roadside.

What to make of all this complex richness of nature and culture around us in the suburbs? How do we live now and understand the lives of those who came before? The floodplain answers me. I simply listen. It's near evening in late February, and the spring peepers and chorus frogs have already started to call in the wet places to our south. The year is moving toward the equinox, and they are mating. The great cycle continues. The peepers prefer the second growth that is abundant in our neighborhood, though they are seldom seen except in damp weather when the inch-long frogs cross the road in our car lights. They congregate to sing in temporary ponds—cutover woodlots, deep truck ruts that hold water—whereas the upland chorus frogs prefer the more extensive wetlands. The chorus frogs always sound to me like someone running his finger over a comb. The field guides say a large chorus of peepers heard from far off sounds like sleigh bells—an odd image for the Deep South. Betsy and I have never heard the sound of sleigh bells except on a Bing Crosby Christmas album, but we both agree we see the comparison.

The intensity of spring peeper calls increases when we reach the corner of Starline and Fairlane. We stop walking and look south, deep into the bottom. "They heard the same sound on early spring nights walking back up from the coast," I say. "They heard them as they were setting up camp on our hillside, making love at night." The dogs even seem lost in the timeless cacophony of the peepers. They pause and lift their noses from the ground. The chorus frogs join in. If any sound can penetrate deep into our shared past, it is this one—the high clear whistles of love from the winter woods.

Stone is of the earth, like us, but it is lasting. We want to marry our short days to stone. . . . But stone is a ticking clock. It is a slow clock, slow enough for us to believe in its consistency.

HOWARD MANSFIELD, *The Bones of the Earth*

Fred's Cache

In William Faulkner's sense of time nothing dies. Time for Faulkner is a place where everything "is" and nothing "was." The southern land for Faulkner is, as Frederick Turner put it in *Spirit of Place,* "a great conservator, repository of all artifacts, of the bone and trinkets, and even the dreams and deeds of the ancestors, for the long, tangled, tragic, and sometimes wildly comic chronicle of the ages could not have been invented for nothing and then thrown into cosmic discard. The spirits of the departed were substantive."

This week I've been thinking about Faulkner and his mythic Mississippi "Big Bottom" and about Terry Ferguson. It's through Terry I most often wander into the complexity of time. Was Faulkner right? What's left of the "was" within this mile circle? Where does time still show itself? Where do the edges of eternity make themselves visible?

Walking with Terry along Lawson's Fork is when I often trip upon the frayed edges where the past and present are sewn together. Terry sees time in the bend of the meandering creek just upstream from the Lake Forest Bridge. Once when visiting that spot, he shaved the bank with a shovel until he could see clearly the horizontal bands of sand, silt, and clay that the creek had deposited in the past. He called this the "erosional bank of the creek, the opposite of the deposition bank." The bands of sediment told him stories of flood "events," some ancient, some historical. He explained how one way to know for sure is to find some carbon or some cultural artifact lodged in the layers, one of Faulkner's trinkets.

In 1968, just downstream from Terry's deposition bank and a quarter mile upstream from our house, Fred Parrish found a "cache" of cultural artifacts, dozens of what at the time he thought were spear points. Fred was raised just up the hill, on the south side of the creek where Lake Forest Drive now crests the ridge top. He says he was out riding a horse in the flood-plain, and he saw one point, just an outline, covered by a thin wash of mud in a puddle. He jumped off his horse and reached for the gray, three-inch stone and quickly realized there were many more, all within a four-foot circle.

Fred is a ball of energy, full of the curiosity of a boy and ready to speculate about soapstone or rivers or arrowheads or anything man-made, growing, or green. He's in his early sixties, retired from work in the accounting office of a now-defunct textile mill, and spends most of his time doing volunteer work for SPACE, the local conservation organization. He is compact with a shock of gray hair and glasses. He's had a bad stutter since childhood, but his elegance of thought and deep learning make you quickly forget about it. "They came up in a scoop," Fred told me one day, recounting that horseback ride, then almost forty years in the past. "That was a link to what was."

Six months after we moved in I invited Terry and his friend, archaeologist Tommy Charles, to lunch at our house. We all sat around the dining room table and talked about the deep past.

Fred came too. We ate chicken salad sandwiches and drank tea, and Fred and I listened as Terry and Tommy laid out the context for Fred's artifacts within the sketchy story of piedmont archaeology.

Terry picked up one point from the box Fred had brought them in and looked at it and said they were probably "preforms," pieces of quarried stone that had been chipped into a rough shape to be fashioned later into finished tools and weapons.

Tommy picked one up and examined it too. He said the rock came from elsewhere—rhyolite or felsite, possibly from the Carolina slate belt a hundred miles to the northeast. After it was quarried and partially chipped it was probably carried here and hidden at different places in a foraging Archaic period band's range, then made into tools as they were needed. "Insurance gear," Terry added.

"Either the man who carried them here forgot them," Tommy continued, "or died before they were used." It was only when Fred spotted them in 1968, thousands of years after they were quarried, that they came back into the play of human imagination again. Tommy was impressed with Fred's find. He said it was maybe the largest cache of preforms he'd seen from the South Carolina piedmont.

For a half-hour or so, prompted by Fred's cache, I listened as Terry and Tommy talked about South Carolina archaeology. Tommy explained how in 1968 the first professional archaeologists were hired at the South Carolina Archaeology Institute. They were from Florida and weren't that interested much in the piedmont area of the state. "Cruddy quartz points? What good are these?" Tommy said. "They wanted those beautiful chert points like you find down in Allendale County."

So not much work has been done up here—South Carolina's landmark sites so far have been Stallings Island, Pine Island, and more recently, the Topper site—all on the Savannah River, and all coastal plain sites mostly focused on Paleo-Indian material.

Artifact hunters, or "arrowhead collectors," have helped some to understand where people lived and traveled on this landscape in the past, but that's really all they've contributed. Terry says it's only "in-place excavation," a fairly recent development in piedmont South Carolina, that reliably dates artifacts that people like Fred pick up on the surface.

Some information comes from systematic surface collections of plowed bottoms, but the best archaeological sites in the South Carolina piedmont are still mostly deeply buried under sediment, and usually they're on private property—hard to locate, hard to access, and expensive to excavate.

Terry and Tommy, both professional archaeologists, know how to place dates on artifacts like the ones we'd laid out on my dining room table, because of work done by other archaeologists over years of fieldwork at sites like the Hardaway site in the North Carolina piedmont, and sites they themselves have worked on recently in the upper piedmont of South Carolina.

"Until about fifty years ago most artifacts were associated with historic tribes like the Cherokee," Terry reminded me. "You have to remember there was no understanding of the Archaic period until the discovery of deep time, of the depth of prehistory, and that wasn't possible until the 1950s when radiocarbon dating became a scientific tool."

Fred had been listening intently. "That corn bottom, out there across the creek? You may have something down there that goes back eight hundred or nine hundred years, something more than meets the eye," he said looking out our back windows into the winter trees. "What Tommy Pierce plants in the spring, that's not the first time that bottom saw corn. Mesoamerican culture was here a long time with squash, beans, and corn."

Terry sat listening and said, "Could be true," as he always

does, "but it would be hard to prove without getting down in there to collect and dig."

"I keep coming back to the edge concept," Fred said, still trying to make his insight clear. He turned to me and offered advice about writing my story. "This edge you're building with your story is where you can step into the past, right out there, still visible. This edge conjures up visions and dreams. It's a stepping-off point. You live right on it here overlooking this bottom."

What Fred spoke was pure poetry, a long way from the lost facts and found truths of our two resident archaeologists, and I'll admit they didn't seem as interested in what Fred was trying to say as they were the artifacts on the table.

One of Fred's favorite books is still *Tribes That Slumber* by Thomas M. N. Lewis and Madeline Kneberg, a beautifully illustrated but according to Terry hopelessly out-of-date book about Indians of the Tennessee River region published in 1958. I imagine that the images dancing in Fred's head while he talked of "conjured visions" were deeply informed by the pictures in *Tribes That Slumber*.

A few pages include a striking series of illustrations showing a pair of dark, disembodied Archaic period hands flaking flint by percussion, another showing the steps for making a fish hook out of a deer toe bone, and another showing a snake's backbone and bobcat teeth strung into necklaces. When Terry speaks of the book being out of date I don't think he means these compelling representations of the material culture of the Archaic period bands. When I talked to him about it he warned me not to take what Lewis and Kneberg say about these people too seriously though. Fifty years of fieldwork is a long time ago in the world of Southeastern archaeology.

But I, like Fred, am susceptible to conjuring. The day before, I'd met Terry at the Patterson site, an archaeology site he was actively studying down at the confluence of Lawson's Fork and the Pacolet River. He needed help to "run lines" with ground-

penetrating radar. It was a beautiful winter day—very warm—
and by the time we started setting up the equipment I'd taken
off my jacket to work in a tee shirt. "Hard to believe it's supposed to be sleeting in the morning," Terry said, looking up at
a blue sky.

The equipment was not easy to set up. Terry had three green
plastic crates it all traveled in. We laid it all out and snapped it
together. The radar unit looked like a big metal detector, and
you pulled it along the ground and clicked a trigger every me-
ter to send down a signal. He'd asked me to bring my wheelbarrow so we could run longer lines. In the wheelbarrow rested the
laptop and the batteries; the wheelbarrow and radar were then
hooked together with two very long heavy duty black cables.

When we were set up we began to run the north/south lines
first. Terry was trying to get more information on what he calls
"the old stream channel" of Lawson's Fork, and so he needed
to run the radar across the field from north to south. On the
screen the data appears as bands of black and white, modeling
what is below the radar unit for a depth of about three me-
ters. It was easy to see the distinct lines as they plunged near
the beginning of what Terry thought was the channel. "There's
something going on here," Terry said. He explained how it was
possible to make an entire 3-D model of the site, but it would
take hundreds of passes with the radar.

A decade before I'd come out to the Patterson site to help
Terry, I had written a poem called "Field Work," about our very
different visions as scientist and poet:

> Terry takes me to his study site,
> a farmer's field near the river,
> and we spend two hours walking
> transects, flagging archaic flakes,
> broken points, and fire-cracked quartz
> hidden in summer-high meadow grass.

I'm tired, sit beneath a pine.
"This is archaeology," he smiles.
Hot sun, the straight lines walked,
shoulder to shoulder, always looking
down. "Not exactly finding Troy."

We've speckled an acre of bottomland
with survey flags, what's left after weather
and plows scrape the old fields clean.

If this is science, it wears me out.
There's too much of the world in it—
I want to walk fields in my mind,
pick up clear spear points, whole pots,
and perfect soapstone bowls.

So I imagine us out past our sweaty field:
four thousand years ago men and women
slept at our feet, made love, dressed
in skins from deer they'd killed, cooked
rabbit stew in soapstone bowls.
That's more like it: imagine that,
a world more interesting than what
was here. Parts more real than wholes.

Parts more real than wholes. That's what I struggled with as I
worked with Terry. It's putting the whole picture together that
takes most of the effort. By temperament I veer more toward
Fred's side of the equation and remind myself that in spite
of my access to scientists like Terry, I need to stay focused on
my own perceptions of this landscape. But fieldwork is hard
to beat. You're outside, there's engagement with a place, and
there's always good conversation.

While we worked at the Patterson site, two black Angus cows
made their way into the field. "I hope they don't eat my flags,"
Terry said.

I looked around. Above me was the old Goldmine Road bed, just below the new roadbed. Now there's a time I know something about, I wanted to say to Terry, the late Holocene—the Time of Pickups out here in the country.

Terry talked a little about time as he pulled the radar unit along. He said that the data we were getting would show us both time and space. "How much of the 'was' is available to the 'is'?" I asked.

I thought again of William Faulkner's view of time—as all "is"—and whether we had been more successful at obliterating the past that day than his generation was.

"It's all time," Terry said, "all knowable to some extent, but as you go deeper in the past the resolution of what you can know diminishes—much like what is happening with the radar."

Terry used as an example a book he is reading about a giant extinction that killed off 95 percent of life on the planet about 250 million years ago. "Until about 1980 no scientists were sure that it had happened. Now it's pretty certain that it did, and we're learning more and more about the events that led to it—possibly a series of volcanoes erupting in Siberia. The dilemma of that extinction now has a plausible explanation."

As we looked at Fred's cache in our dining room I tried to go as deeply as I could and hold onto the "resolution" as Terry had called it in the field. "Life is so short and now it is flying past me," a friend had written this week from Charlottesville, Virginia, where she grew up and has now returned. "I walk among ghosts every day. I hear them, feel them, see them, and I know, soon me too. Oddly, I don't mind the feeling, only seeing the facts."

"The hard stone fact," writer James Kilgo in his essay "Indian Games" once called an Archaic period point he found on the Savannah River. "Everything about it meant business." There was no doubt what these points had been shaped to do—bring down some beast or skin one out once dead. I could almost see the scene, right out the January window. As I looked at the points laid out on my dining room table it didn't take me long to leap from Jim Kilgo's "hard stone fact" to my own imagination, only partially informed by what Tommy and Terry had already told us. To hold the past in check, that was the challenge. In the spaces deep time offers, there are so many opportunities to make up a world. One of the only ways to adjust the present to the past is to ask questions, plenty of them.

In a few minutes we walked up the creek from our house and cut over past Tommy Pierce's duck ponds and intersected Fairlane Drive where it T-bones into Lake Forest. We made the turn north, the creek at our backs; Fred showed us where he'd scooped up that cache of blades next to Cold Water Branch. Once again, he told the story of riding a horse through the bottom before it was settled. His family had been pioneers up on Woodburn Road, moving from Converse Heights in the 1950s, "Going east, to a place with land, a barn, and the promise of chickens, water spilling down a hillside, feeding Lawson's Fork."

Fred and I stood and listened as Tommy and Terry looked around. We speculated more about the distant past that Fred's points helped define and what other knowledge of it might still be deeply buried in the fields. Tommy pointed north and talked about how the "secondary terrace above that spring," a flat place half the size of a football field right in the backyards of several of the Lake Forest houses, could have been a site for a village—water nearby, south-facing to get the good winter sun. If Fred's story of finding the artifacts was accurate, it could have been occupied for ten thousand years—possibly a seasonal camp for Paleo-Indian and Archaic period hunters and gatherers, a Woodlands village, or a Cherokee camp. What we know of piedmont archaeology in these early periods has been learned from sites like this, ancient "living surfaces" and the artifacts associated with them buried under alluvial deposits.

That time with Terry, Tommy, and Fred was the first I slowed down enough to take it all in, the whole circle and how it all stretched out before me right there at the corner of Lake Forest and Fairlane—from the paleo-past to the current suburbs. Do my suburban neighbors have any idea they're living in country first settled ten thousand years ago? Do they care that in their backyards are possibly buried the hearths of lodges warmed by red oak and white oak cut from the very slopes they think they now "own?" Does it matter that they don't know about their Archaic period neighbors?

If Faulkner is right about time, then it does. My afternoon with Terry, Tommy, and Fred suggests that all around and under this suburban frontier sleeps Faulkner's ever-present "is," a "long, tangled, tragic, and sometimes wildly comic chronicle of the ages," and where better to track it than right at home?

> Suburbia is America. . . . Today our politics are ruled by
> the suburbs; suburbia's agenda—that is, issues bearing on
> the well-being of families with children, around which the
> suburbs still revolve—is now America's.
>
> MICHAEL POLLAN, "The Triumph of Burbopolis"

Suburban Renewal

When we built our life in the borderland between Spartanburg's stalled east-side suburbs and a few threatened scraps of
forests, I knew we were buying into America's suburban agenda.
I knew our dream house would not be some rural expanse
where corn is a cash crop or in some dark wilderness deep
enough for bears. I know that, like it or not, our neighbors
wouldn't just be the wild turkey, white-tailed deer, bobcat, gray
fox, short tail shrew, star-nosed mole. If we were to have a block
party we'd have to invite others besides the black rat snakes, the
salamanders, the gray and green tree frogs. We're surrounded.
There's suburban settlement on every side, with only one escape route, the river running like a wild renegade through the
middle of it all.

It's no different here than most places people settle and call
home these days. There aren't many people today living in frontier cabins or *Little House on the Prairie* homesteads. The last
half of the twentieth century saw the rise of the suburbs every-

where, an invention for building an American dream outside the city center, and the east side of Spartanburg is that suburban dream writ large. All the old agricultural land—all someone's homestead at some point in the deep past—has mostly been replaced with streets in grids, square lots of equal size, the orientation of houses parallel to the road. Out front an unbroken greensward lawn stretches from street to street, punctuated only by a few ornamental trees and garden-center shrubs. These nearby signs of a forty-year suburban revolution have brought about the passing of the agricultural landscape of the old South. In spite of our "green" design and our eye toward sustainability, our house is suburban "in-fill," and the building of it in the first decade of the twenty-first century is at best only a period on a development sentence first composed by community planners long ago.

The suburbs are more than houses on lots and jokes about sameness. *Suburban Nation*, a book about the rise of sprawl by Andres Duany, Elizabeth Plater-Zyberk, and Jeff Speck, argues that suburbia is in our heads. It's an idea as strongly planted in Baby Boomers as democracy. We late twentieth-century creatures think suburban. We express this worldview in terms of the five units of suburban growth—tracts of houses, office parks, institutions like schools or churches, strip malls, and roads, lots of roads. The measure of suburbia's success is housing starts. When we drive out of our "resident clusters" to shop or go to school (for one of the laws of suburbia is separation), we drive through a built world projected by our minds, constructed by our dollars, and protected by our laws.

In spite of talk of LEED certification and maintaining a wooded lot we've done little to shift this suburban paradigm with our choice to build here. We are still part of the process, a family whose agenda is still the same as the majority of the country's. Le Corbusier, the French architect who was one of the godfathers of what we now call sprawl, was a prophet for the world we've settled in: "The cities will be part of the country. . . . We shall use up tires, wear out road surfaces and gears, consume oil and gasoline." I'm not proud of it, but it's a reality I'm prepared to accept.

The writer Michael Pollan has a softer view of suburbia, or what in a *New York Times Magazine* article in 2000 he called "The Triumph of Burbopolis." Pollan grew up in the northeastern suburbs and, though he fled them for rural New England, he sees their triumph as not all bad. The year 1960 was a sort of watershed for the suburban nation according to Pollan. By that year one-third of the country was suburban, one-third city, one-third rural. In 1960 the city still ruled, even if from afar, through cultural attitudes, manners, and ideas. The rural had long ceded any chance of influencing the direction of America, though the future belonged to the suburbs.

Yes, we have become a "suburban nation," he says, since over half of Americans now live in them. But "Suburbia's cultural power is harder to see," and "that may be because it is everywhere, indistinguishable from the air we breathe." And how does that cultural power show up in our midst? Because of the suburbs America has become a more informal place, and it has also embraced a certain weird "ironic detachment" from land, community, any sort of seriousness.

In addition to the suburban agenda we agreed to in principle when we moved to Forest Hills we also were given a ten-page document of binding covenants we could not violate. Mobile homes are prohibited. We would set our house back from Tempo Court at least fifty feet; we could not construct a garage that opened onto the street; there would be no metal buildings, no chickens, goats, cows, or horses on our lot. We could not subdivide, and our house would have at least two thousand square feet of heated space.

Before we arrived our neighbors had bought or built their houses according to the conventional brick styles of the sixties—colonial, ranch, or split-level. The Levitts, who pioneered mass-produced homes in Levittown at midcentury, would recognize the streets leading down to Tempo Court, our cul-de-sac.

If home is a place of comfort, of ease, in some ways we've failed completely by moving out here. Not a day goes by in which I don't squirm in my seat and think about what could be. What if our neighbors and we suddenly stopped being suburban? What if we all saw the silliness of lawns and chemicals and exotic flora? What if we closed a few roads and let the grass reclaim them? What if reports of black bears and coyotes gave us all joy instead of dread? What if trails were welcome and trespass became a word as ancient as royalty?

One warm late winter day I sat around on our deck with a friend, staring into the floodplain. We drank too much beer and concocted an ambitious national plan to recover the suburbs at our backs, a sort of "suburban renewal" program. What would happen if Congress were suddenly invaded with green thinkers like the new political radicals, and we threw as much money at the suburbs as the social liberals did toward "urban renewal" programs of the 1970s?

We could spend billions buying and tearing down the ranch houses that were built in riparian zones along all the rivers and creeks, great and small. We could spend billions more tax dollars breaking up with islands of woodland the artificial short grass prairies, the suburban lawns. It was no more silly an idea than the B-1 bomber or tobacco subsidies or No Child Left Behind!

Then we could pump another round of block grants into replacing crape myrtles and flowering pear trees with trillium and false Solomon's seal, foam flower, and native piedmont trees like dogwoods and hackberry and hickory. Forget beach renourishment. Give the suburbs billions for topsoil replenishment!

"And billions for clinics to teach Joe Suburbs like us to recycle our cereal boxes!" my friend ranted.

"Stations could be set up in strip mall parking lots where suburbanites could bring in their uprooted exotics to be shredded into mulch in exchange for something native and fine," I said. "It could be a revolution! The whole world watching! Finally, back to the garden!"

But I sobered up the next day and began thinking again about the realities of this place we'd moved into. They were actually more interesting than the fantasies. Yes, it's true we live in the suburbs, but what's really compelling about where we've settled is that big floodplain out back. We're attached by our rear property line to space that could never in a thousand years be confused with suburbia, and it's in that space that I find the most challenges to my ideas about our neighbors and their property.

About a month before we moved in I was working on some landscaping in the backyard. I heard a four-wheeler pass, and I stormed down to the creek. I have an irrational dislike for recreational four-wheelers, a dislike I also extend to snowmobiles and jet skis. All three are the same genus to me. I see four-wheelers not as an alternative to horses, as ranchers use them out west, but as loud, destructive toys that suburbanites use to invade the last wild territory around their lots. They roar in packs through the backcountry, bent on throwing mud and crushing any native vegetation that grows up in their trails. They deepen trail ruts in a season. They roar through creek crossings, silting down the flow. Mountain bikes can explore the same territory with less damage, and bikes don't use gasoline. Hiking is an even better alternative. What good can come of a four-wheeler, a trail, and the deep instinct to wreak havoc?

We'd been told the Pierces had finally put a stop to the once-heavy four-wheeler traffic a decade ago, so when I first heard one of the machines go past, I figured it was a renegade suburbanite, and I would put him in his place, even though it wasn't my land he was crossing. I ran down the trail to where the interloper was off his machine cutting a large log that had fallen across the trail. "Hey *you*!" I yelled over the chainsaw, but the dismounted four-wheeler wasn't aware I was behind him. "Hey!" I yelled when the log had finally fallen to the ground. I startled the man with the saw, and he turned slowly to face me. He was not happy. He was a young guy in full-length Carhart overalls, a ball cap, and wraparound sunglasses. "This is Pierce land," I yelled. "You're trespassing!"

"This is *my* land," the man with the chainsaw said, stepping toward me. "I'm Trey Pierce."

We somehow survived the incident on speaking terms. Though more than a little irritated because I had startled him, Trey seemed to appreciate the effort to keep the four-wheeler traffic down. I can now distinguish between the green Pierce four-wheeler with the basket on the back and those that are not. The Pierces move at a reasonable rate of speed on their machines, and always there's a huge friendly lab running along with them. Absolutes, even concerning four-wheelers, are hard to maintain in a world with neighbors.

But these problems are at the heart of communities. Figuring out where your business stops and where someone else takes up theirs is a task we've been at for millions of years, and I haven't really had much practice at it. Twenty years on the road made me good at traffic laws and the courtesies governing lane changes on interstate highways, but that didn't really help much when it came to living next to people. How must this incident have looked to Trey Pierce? First of all, this crazy tree-hugger college professor buys a couple of lots and then confronts him on his own trail as he cuts through one of *his* downed trees with a chainsaw. It must have seemed outlandish, and looking back, I'm glad Trey didn't just fence off the whole parcel for good.

Robert Frost leads off his second collection *North of Boston* with "Mending Wall," maybe the best thing anyone's ever written about the complexity of neighborliness. "Something there is that doesn't love a wall," Frost warns us. But there are no rustic New England stonewalls here. There are not even any fences between "them" and us. There is only the abstract boundary of a courthouse document filed away across town. We're glad for such uncertainty as we walk some evenings with the dogs on their land next to the creek.

Are good neighbors those who leave the values of others alone, or challenge them? How do we live in a place without loving it all, well beyond what our deeds define as ours? How do we not look out our back windows and want the creek that crawls through the floodplain to run clean and protected from vandals who see it otherwise? These questions pool in the eddy now obscured from my view by the dark branches of the winter trees and lead me on into more explorations. My story takes me circling out well beyond my own property lines.

This weekend I've been digging postholes and pouring quickset cement, expanding what we hope is a four-wheeler-proof trail along the back of our property. I've been building my own fences. There are some teenagers from deeper in the neighborhood who have recently pushed over river birch saplings at one end of the trail to gain access to our property with their infernal machine.

When I first heard them I rushed out on the deck as they hauled down our short stretch of trail on their muddy black machine. A full squad of Huns couldn't make me madder.

I always feel like Mr. Wilson in *Dennis the Menace* after such encounters. When I come inside I try to settle my nerves by assuring myself the offense of these trespassing teenage four-wheelers will not land them far down in Hades. They are teenagers doing what teens have always done—getting out of the house, acting out a mild version of "Born to be Wild" right down the street on somebody else's property.

"Trespassing? At least they aren't robbing the Little Cricket," one of my friends said, laughing, when I complained about the four-wheelers on our trail.

The autumn we built our house, I heard a racket on the trail and walked down to find two kids in a jeep setting a winch on a tree trunk that was blocking their way to the once wild territory behind our property. They had a chain saw on the seat.

"Hey," I asked. "What are you doing?"

"Oh," they said, climbing into the jeep for a getaway. "We're just leaving."

"If you're just leaving," I said, "Then why were you hooking your winch to that tree?"

They smiled and 'fessed up, told me they wanted to cut their way back to the creek to go four wheeling before an annual football game with a crosstown rival. "It's a tradition," they said.

"It might be a tradition, but this is our backyard," I said. "I now own this trail."

"Somebody owns this land?" they asked, sweeping their arms around to encompass all the open space as if it were the Alaskan backcountry, hoping the world behind our house was their recreational commons.

Soon after that funny encounter I planted a line of hefty six-by-six posts two feet apart to cut our trail off to large vehicles. I mounted a neat white and green sign at the trailhead stating our preferences for recreational use: "No motorized vehicles or firearms."

I know, I know. Ease up. Maybe I should work on my own tolerance levels. Maybe when I hear the sound of a posse of four-wheelers hauling down the sewer right-of-way behind our house I should try first to lower my blood pressure. Read a book. Put in earplugs. Subscribe to *All-Terrain Monthly* and read it on the deck.

Our blockade stopped the jeeps, but those pesky little four-wheelers still come right on in. I'm hoping this latest string of posts will slow them down as well. Should I negotiate with my inner Mr. Wilson? I'm not giving up. I prefer my backyard quiet.

Why care? Just think of it as my small way of rolling back the Age of Gasoline or renewing the suburbs. Aren't many of those teenagers out there riding on four-wheelers overweight? Shouldn't they be walking anyway?

Patterns of settlement, once launched, tend to have great staying power: The sites of most of the cities in this very young country were all chosen long ago, some of them back in the seventeenth century. How can any of us see to it that the fully grown America we're already preparing for—or the America after that—will continue to make available to people the kind of richly varied and nurturing experiences people have always needed?

TONY HISS, *The Experience of Place*

Across the Creek and into the Suburbs

One Saturday in March I finally called my friends Manning and Mary Speed Lynch and said I'd be over in half an hour to look for the colonial roadbed—the Old Georgia Road—that runs through their property in the Glenn Forest subdivision. Manning and Mary Speed built their contemporary house on the site of the old Bagwell plantation house on the other side of the creek, and I'd wanted to walk their large wooded lot since I started thinking about the circle. The Lynch property is a place shaggy with history.

So I cut across the circle, from the center to the southeast edge, dropping down to the creek, climbing the valley on the other side, and ending up on the high ridge a mile away. I was out to feel the long span of human occupation under my bike tires. I was hungry for a landscape I could trace through oral histories and property transfers. I wanted to wade back through the present into the recent and shallow past, to explore the beginnings of our community's recorded history.

My quest was what writer Howard Mansfield calls, strangely enough, "the unnaming of things" in *The Bones of the Earth*. What he means is that sometimes the present is like old wallpaper we need to pull away to get back to older relationships with the land. It was not the current road names and subdivisions I sought. I know them. My plan was to uncover the colonial past lost beneath the modern day real estate plats of Oak Creek Plantation and Glenn Forest. I didn't expect to find kinship (my people are mostly from eastern North Carolina or the mountains to the west), but I did anticipate a great deal of cultural empathy.

I pulled my old mountain bike out of the furnace room and headed down below our house to where the trail runs east/west along the creek. It's thick with trees down there in the creek bottom, and it's only on the trail that you can make any progress at all. Just upstream, a narrow ruined bridge from the days this area was a farm crosses over Lawson's Fork and heads up an old rutted road right-of-way. It's all Pierce land down there. By road it's five or six miles over to Manning's, so the shortcut reduces it to a mile or so, though technically it's trespassing. I don't make a habit of trespassing on Tommy's land, but I decided, if caught, I'd cite the old adage about forgiveness being easier to come by than permission, and I set off.

It was raining when I left, just a little, a raw South Carolina winter rain. The muddy trail crosses Lawson's Fork next to the sewer treatment plant on what's left of an old wooden bridge patched together with mismatched planks. I stopped on the bridge to look at the thirty-foot-wide creek, and what I saw, upstream and down, was a meandering shallow piedmont waterway with deadwood breaking the current and shards of trash caught in the trees from the last high water. Trees, mostly river birches, leaned out at impossible angles, their dark trunks reflected in the water. Some rested in the channel. Anything beautiful about the creek came from the angle of the light, the surface mirroring the filigree of the branches in eddies and flat stretches of moving water. The colors in the stream, shimmering as it flowed, were greens, grays, browns, and a strange silver I couldn't locate in anything above. There was a slight murmur like blood passing through a valve as Lawson's Fork searched out its channel downstream through its remaining ancient floodplain. It smelled slightly of chlorine followed by the malt-thick odor of decay.

As I paused on the bridge I heard the treatment plant's processing tanks in high gear, and I realized the organic smell was the plant's sludge ponds—that earthy odor that often is picked up by a breeze and wafted all the way downstream to our house on the ridge. The chlorine smell was from the last step in the treatment process where the gas is added to the wastewater to kill any remaining pathogens before it passes back into the stream.

On the other side of the bridge I stopped and stared down into the ditch that channels the release, the "effluent," back into Lawson's Fork. Twenty percent of the flow in our creek is outfall from this plant, so I don't complain much about its presence upstream. Today there is more pressure from the surrounding affluent neighborhoods, so the Sewer and Water District has launched a building campaign for relocating the outfall to the neighboring watershed and enclosing the treatment process here so the odor will be eliminated, or at least diminished. I'll miss the flow when it's gone. I like to watch the creek flow, and the higher it is the better. "Not in my backyard," is the rallying cry of most neighborhoods now when it comes to sewage or trash, but this plant has been in operation since 1938, when most of my whole circle was agricultural or forested and immune to the aesthetic differences with sewer plants. As Graham Rich, the former director of the Sewer and Water District, liked to say of the waste management business, "Trees make the best neighbors."

I've always liked the close kinship in sound between "effluence" and "affluence." They both suggest water, flow, whether it's wealth or treated waste. While I sat looking into the ditch I pondered the miracle of waste treatment in a modern city like Spartanburg: all our foulest waste comes into this plant in a forty-two-inch pipe, and somehow, only a day or so later, the wastewater is returned to the creek government-certified and clean enough to sustain life in Lawson's Fork. It's a miracle of communal action, and I blessed the hardworking employees of the plant as I passed by.

I tried hard to make a similar metaphor out of wealth—affluence—and decided that through investment and philanthropy wealth flows back into a community. I knew there were problems with this metaphor if I pushed it too far, but it would have to do for the moment.

Climbing on up the hill in low gear I headed almost due south, kicking up gravel and bits of asphalt from decades ago when this straight-shot road from ridge to ridge was paved to the creek and the old bridge there. The air had a bite to it, and I stopped to pull one more layer from my pack and look at my topo with the circle on it to get my bearings. I was a little southwest of our house, and the sewer plant was directly to my west, and just beyond it, across a big ridge where my brother-in-law lived with his family, was the Country Club of Spartanburg. Exploring that territory, one of the wealthiest neighborhoods in the city, would have to wait for another day.

I was gaining altitude, maybe seventy or eighty feet above the floodplain, when I passed a spot where I caught a view of Tommy's farmland on my left. It looked a little like a scene from the Appalachians, with the big creek-bottom field spiked with dead corn and the creek itself sweeping past just beyond. I knew our house was up there in the trees beyond the creek, but I couldn't see it from where I stopped. There was too much distance and too many trees, even without their leaves.

Riding on, I squeezed through Tommy's locked gate, finally found some level ground and passed the old folks' home on my right. It's a two-story modern facility, built several decades ago, and is constructed of fake stucco and institutional landscaping: spindly crape myrtles, turf lawns, mulch. It's not an unpleasant place, but it makes me sad to pass by. I wish those old people had a nice porch to sit on and watch the creek flowing a few hundred yards down the hill from them. Instead, their neighbor, the sewer treatment plant, has the creek-front property. I'm sure the sweet smell of the perking sludge is something the old folks know well.

At the entrance to the old folks' home I finally crossed Country Club Road almost where the old Spartanburg-Glendale electric trolley changed sides of the road from 1900 until 1935. For three decades the trolley crossed the road and disappeared behind a knoll. One old resident told me this Country Club Road crossing was the "demarcation zone" between the mill village of Glendale a mile down the road and one of Spartanburg's first little subdivisions, Ben Avon, less than a mile up the road toward town. It was a place marked by fights and taunts. There's no trace of the trolley now except the ghost in the first street name inside Oak Creek Plantation: Trolley Car Way.

I pedaled across the busy two-lane road and on into Oak Creek, a large, upscale subdivision developed in the 1980s, and "affluence" enveloped me. I needed all my gears to climb the hill up Bagwell Farm Road. In the 1980s Gertrude Bagwell, the last surviving heir of the Bagwells, sold a three-hundred-acre portion of their seventeen-hundred-acre nineteenth-century cotton plantation to develop Oak Creek. She's buried now in the family cemetery in the center of the subdivision, and it was my hope that Manning could show me her grave.

I headed up through Oak Creek Plantation and crossed into

Glenn Forest, a sister subdivision that developed a little later than Oak Creek. It was also created out of Bagwell property, though it was just outside the preferred school-district line. Because of its location, it's taken almost ten years for Glenn Forest to build out.

Glenn Forest is a pleasant place too. The houses and lots are often smaller, but the property values are often a little higher than in Oak Creek. There are no green-space belts separating the streets, and the building was done "lot line to lot line," so the place has much more of the feel of sprawl belts around most southern cities. Even the Glenn Forest Lake is a little smaller than one in the earlier Oak Creek Plantation.

Soon after I passed into Glenn Forest I turned down Dare's Ferry Road, and I could see Manning's driveway at the end of the cul-de-sac. Manning and Mary Speed had bought their lot in Glenn Forest before things took off. Their children, like ours, go to the Spartanburg Day School, so school district lines weren't quite so important. Manning is a contractor, and his bread and butter is what the industry calls "affordable housing" out in the county—reasonably priced houses on smaller lots— but his personal taste in houses and landscape is a lot like ours, a custom house on a big wooded lot.

I entered the drive that circles in front of the house around an old chimney from the nineteenth century. The large tract, originally set aside as the location for a clubhouse for the subdivision, is heavily wooded and was the site of the 1860 Bagwell antebellum mansion that burned in the 1970s. The house Manning and Mary Speed built is very contemporary and disappears into the woods around it, painted hues of grey and dark brown. More Hilton Head than Spartanburg, the Lynch home is secluded and buffered from the smaller lots of Glenn Forest by seven acres of big oaks, cedars, and dense undergrowth.

Manning met me at the door. A rusted fountain from Mary Speed's old family home bubbled behind us in a brick patio on one side of the entryway. Tall and jovial, Manning wore a down vest and hiking boots and looked more like the owner of a fly-fishing business than a builder. He pointed out the fountain and said he'd seen a great blue heron in the pool several times recently, trying to eat his fish.

I explained my project and showed him the topo with the circle on it and how the Bagwells were ground zero for a sort of gentrified agricultural life in the circle that had lasted until the end of the nineteenth century. Manning said he and Mary Speed had always wondered about the history of the place and looked forward to whatever I came up with. We walked out to the side of the house, and he showed me several artifacts from the old Bagwell place—a beautiful stacked stone wall with three stone steps in the middle of it and the old roadbeds that came through his property from the south. "That's about all that's left," he said. He'd put up a barrier to keep people from driving down the old road bed. The old route was so prominent somebody might still drive it in spite of the small saplings that had grown up.

We walked to the west side of the house, and Manning showed me where an old two-story Bagwell building had stood when he bought the property in the early 1990s. There was nothing left but a few foundation stones and pieces of tin. Manning picked up an old brick, and I could see the gravel in it—maybe hand-formed right here on site, baked in a real plantation kiln. Just to my right, down a slope, I could see what was the distinct outline of the old roadbed continuing down to the shoals—the Old Georgia Road—where it's said the colonials had skirmished with the Tories in 1780. It was what I'd hoped to find.

After we finished our tour around the house we sat for a half hour near the fountain and looked at the old maps of the area I'd collected, one dating back to 1791 that showed the colonial roads passing near Manning's front yard. Both of us were drawn toward the large tracts of undeveloped land just east of Glendale, but for slightly different reasons. I told Manning I worried that what was left of rural Spartanburg County would develop badly.

"All that green space will someday get filled up with tiny subdivisions and trailer parks," I said, moving my hand just outside the circle on the topo and on down Lawson's Fork.

Manning shared his builder's optimism—"It's a different time now." Floodplain regulations since the 1970s had already controlled the destruction of what I loved most—the really wild places like the floodplains and the land right up next to the creeks.

We left my mountain bike at Manning's house and rode in his big white contractor's pickup up to the Bagwell cemetery. It's a large quiet piece of property, protected on all sides by mature hardwoods. We parked the truck on the street and walked through the woods on a muddy, gravel two-track to reach the "burying grounds," as they used to be called. The spot has an old-fashioned feel about it, a traditional family cemetery now in the middle of the suburbs, buffered by a small patch of returning forest.

It's quite beautiful, with a stout black fence around it and "Bagwell" spelled out in metal script on the heavy wrought iron gate. Within that was the original old, fieldstone wall. What really catches your eye though is a line of newer white marble stones that were put up a few decades ago, replacing the original stones for the central Bagwell line from William forward to the generation that sold the land for development. Some of the original stones that are left show the signs of years of vandalism—three stones knocked over, broken off. There are graves outside the fence, mostly marked with fieldstones. Slaves or neighbors? A huge old hemlock broods over it all and keeps out the light even in winter.

As we stood and looked down at this line of Spartanburg County Bagwells, I thought about how fine it would be to have a hiking/biking trail that follows the route of the Old Georgia Road, and I lamented to myself the fact of its passing as a public right-of-way, lost now among the plats of Glenn Forest. I didn't bring this up with Manning, since I had a feeling that with our similarities and sympathies this was where we would disagree— how much access the world should have to private property. So I kept quiet and instead told him what else I'd discovered about the first Bagwell on this land.

William Bagwell, the man who built the first house on Manning's place, came to Spartanburg County during the American Revolution. He'd migrated down from Hillsboro, North Carolina, where he was born in 1762. He'd probably traveled the Old Georgia Road from Charlotte.

During my research I'd tracked down a Bagwell cousin in North Carolina who was willing to talk. He'd said that family lore had William fighting as a very young man under the command of Nathaniel Greene in the Revolution, though as one local historian pointed out, "so did every other southerner." There were several major battles fought close by, including the Battle of Cowpens less than twenty miles northeast of the Bagwell Plantation, though William Bagwell's name does not show up on rolls for either Cowpens or King's Mountain. There was one skirmish in 1780 called The Battle of Wofford's Iron Works that happened on what would, after the war, become Bagwell land. Though family lore has William settling here in 1790 he does not show up in the federal census for that year.

Standing at the old Bagwell family cemetery looking over the graves of four generations of Bagwells, I told Manning what one pallbearer remembered about the day of the funeral of Gertrude, the last of the line. It was rainy and muddy, and there was concern about whether the mourners would even be able to reach the family plot.

Gertrude's generosity extended even beyond the grave. An architect in town has told me that he did a little work for her when she returned to Spartanburg. Gertrude had a nice oriental rug in the hallway of the Mills Avenue house, and he told her several times he admired it. After she died he got a call from a New York lawyer saying Miss Bagwell had left it to him. It's still in his entry hall a few miles away.

When the Bagwells died they were planted for eternity there in piedmont clay in a hidden family cemetery in the midst of suburbia. What was lost when large parcels of Bagwell land were transformed and they no longer grew corn, farming only middle-class values instead? What happens when the row crops give way to rows of houses like Glenn Forest and Oak Creek Plantation? What's abandoned when the tenant houses fall into the blackberry brambles and are soon replaced by real estate plats and increasing property values?

One thing's for sure. There's no turning back the land-use clock. Once land makes the transition on the tax rolls from agriculture to residential it's unlikely that it will ever be agricultural again. An old farm can become an old field and an old field can, in a generation, become a forest, but an old suburb simply becomes an older and older suburb.

In the land-use game a cemetery like the Bagwells' is often a safe haven. Most people leave graveyards alone unless they happen to fall in the path of highways or end up under lakes. I took in the white headstones one more time in their long stark row before the rusty gate clanged shut behind us, and I left the Bagwell cemetery confident that Gertrude and her kin will rest soundly in their ten-acre sanctuary as long as there are lawyers to keep the developers away.

After we left the cemetery Manning drove me down the hill to a lot that looks out over the Glenn Forest Lake. The terrain is steep there, and the lake is formed by what was called Spring Branch on a Bagwell plat I'd found from 1912. The terrain falls sharply to reach the level of Lawson's Fork in the valley below. Another contractor, who had worked in the subdivision before the lake was built, told me there were two nice little waterfalls hidden now under the lake's surface. Once, it was a "beauty spot" that many in the valley would visit in the hot months of the summer to cool off, now drowned by the impoundment of the subdivision lake. Waterfall or lake? Which is more beautiful? It's easy to argue either way, though I find myself wishing the waterfall could someday fall again through the mountain laurel and dog hobble that I know would grow around it.

We stood next to Manning's truck. Several more lots were being cleared for new houses. We looked downstream toward the confluence of Four Mile Branch and Lawson's Fork less than a quarter mile away across County Club Road. Below the dam the creek is backed up in an extensive beaver wetlands. From a different perspective, driving down Country Club Road, I'd been able to see that it's a wild little finger of land, a soggy kingdom of cattail, bullfrogs, and woodpeckers working all the dead trees, all the way from the road crossing upstream to the Glenn Forest dam. I wondered out loud if the subdivision owns this property below us in the creek bottom. Manning confirmed. It's floodplain, unbuildable, and so quickly falls off the radar.

The return of wildness to the landscape within the circle is one of the things that surprises me. By the 1830s most of what we could see from the overlook was under cultivation, and there soon would be an emerging textile industry downstream in Bivingsville, just out of sight on the location of a steeper Lower Lawson's Fork shoals.

The Bivingsville (later changed to Glendale) mill site was less than a mile from the old Bagwell house, and as the industry expanded it would have become more and more of a center of interest. Some of the Bivingsville land on the south side of Lawson's Fork could very well have belonged to William Bagwell, though the village developed mostly on the north side of the creek on property that most likely belonged to his cousin Littleton.

Manning had work to do at home, so we climbed in the pick-up and headed back to his house, where my bike was stashed among the remnants of the Bagwell farm. As we drove I thought about Thoreau. In 1861, less than a year before he died, Henry David wrote in his journal: "What are the natural features which make a township handsome? A creek, with its waterfall and meadows, a lake, a hill, a cliff or individual rocks, a forest, and ancient trees standing singly. Such things are beautiful; they have a high use which dollars and cents never represent."

I kept quiet about Henry David Thoreau, though I thought Manning would probably agree with his goals of "making a township handsome." Manning's got a big "Protect Property Rights" sticker on his truck, so I don't think his property would be opened up anytime soon for Thoreau's "higher uses" no matter how much convincing I could do. There should be clear borders and boundaries, Manning might say, between what is mine and what is yours, and much of what we call civil society in the South is based on keeping those boundaries clear. Or as Frost put it, "I am pine and he is apple orchard."

As I rode back to Manning's place I held onto a deep nostalgia for the nineteenth-century agricultural world of the Bagwell farm before the coming of the twentieth-century subdivisions. I've only been able to construct a fragmented story of this one Bagwell family line sprawling over a few hundred acres of hillside and ridge top for almost two centuries. How many other stories are lost around me like the route of the rutted bed of the Old Georgia Road?

Manning seems comfortable with the present, the relentless pace of change of the piedmont landscape from abandoned farm field, to second- and third-growth forest, then finally to subdivision. He's a builder, and so it's his job to build, to anticipate new beginnings, fresh starts. I'm a writer, and it's my job to reflect—to call into question change and progress, to wonder where new beginnings lead and what drove them in the first place.

The land I've been exploring was worn out by the end of the nineteenth century. No amount of nostalgic reflection can replace the foot of topsoil eroded by poor farming practices and washed downstream on Lawson's Fork. Many nineteenth-century deeds in piedmont courthouses have stamped across them GTT—for "gone to Texas," where the farmers abandoned their piedmont farms and left to a better life out West.

The Bagwells held ownership until 1970, and the land stayed open fields. A friend of mine grew up in Glendale, and in the late 1940s and 1950s he remembers hunting rabbits with a .22 rifle on the old Bagwell place. It was considered a sort of commons, made so by absentee land owners. It was a perfect landscape for small game hunting—broom sedge fields turned burnt gold in the fall, a big rogue pine or two, and the hazy tree lines in the distance. It was like a calendar from an old southern childhood. He and his buddies were also members of the Glendale Brave Boys Club, and initiation included stealing a chip from a gravestone in the Bagwell cemetery between dark and daylight and coming back the next day to match it up.

Retired professor B. G. Stephens remembers visiting the old Bagwell home site. The "big house" was unoccupied, but it was still full of family possessions. There were no locks on the doors, and the boys would sneak in and walk around. There was family furniture in all the rooms—an old spinning wheel and even a box of silver dollars. "We never touched anything. I was amazed that nobody took it all," he recalls.

They'd go out back and climb into the attic of the old log cabin and rummage through boxes of financial documents from the old farm—ledgers, canceled checks, accounting sheets for the sale of corn and silage. "Old man Bagwell kept everything," my friend said, reflecting back on his childhood. "I wish I would have known how valuable such a stash of papers really was."

By the 1980s, when Gertrude returned from New York, the old house had been gone for two decades, burned down in the early 1960s. Maybe it was kids with less concern for the place than these Glendale boys had who explored it. So much of history has been lost to fire, but even more has been lost to the American dream.

Manning took me back up to his house, the site of the old Bagwell place. He dropped me off to get my bike, and I rode out through the subdivision. I crossed Old Ironworks Road, Old House Road, and stared up it toward the entrance to the cemetery where Gertrude rested with her family safely behind a fence bought with the proceeds from the sale of the farm. She was a good businesswoman to get concessions from the developers—celebrating the sense of history, retaining a sizable buffer around the cemetery, and securing the site of the old home place as one large tract.

What makes this a place worth remembering? Certainly not the suburban houses built on small lots, landscaped with predictable shrubs set out in patterns recognizable from *Southern Living*. If anything real survives of this place it probably hunkers in the few acres of land saved from the subdivisions—the two parcels Gertrude insisted be set aside, the bottomland along the creeks not flooded by the two lakes and the ragged divisions of scrub and timber set between rows of houses in Oak Creek.

I took strange comfort in the changes around me as Manning dropped me at my bike and I pedaled up the streets of Glenn Forest and Oak Creek. No one there concerned themselves with such questions. They were all at home, comfortable without my ideas about property and history. I was the intruder. I was alone in my nostalgia for a lost agricultural landscape buried for decades by loans and plats and bulldozers under durable streets and foundations and houses.

As I pedaled, the past seemed invisible, but the present and future were still being cultivated all around me by builders like Manning and dreamers like me. It was downhill all the way out of Oak Creek, and my bike didn't stop coasting.

Any path can become the path if attended to with care,
without preconceptions, informed by knowledge, and open
to surprise.

CHET RAYMO, *The Path*

The Upper Shoals

The upper shoals have a wildness about them—big trees, exposed rock, and falling water. I like to walk down there with the
dogs and pretend we live far from town surrounded by nothing
but forest. The path along the creek through the floodplain is
not ours. It's owned by the Milliken family, one of the wealthiest
in the United States. We find what refuge we can among their
abundant acres.

One spring Saturday I walked down from our house, and
I could hear the upper shoals before I could see them. Two
ridges pinch in tight there a quarter mile above Glendale, and
most of the creek rushes through a narrow, fifty-yard-long channel blasted in the gray bedrock for an undershot water wheel
when the shoals were what was called "a mill seat," a place where
falling water was captured for power. The old man-made channel is a great kayaking spot, and our boys, when younger, loved
to float down a half-mile below our house and "run the chute."

The dogs knew exactly where we were going. Ellie Mae was

off-leash, and Toby trailed his in the mud. They waited at the shoals while I recovered a big plank I'd stashed in the woods. We use it to bridge some open water flowing on the north side of the rocky expanse. Toby went across easily. Ellie Mae always has to be coaxed across the narrow board.

Soon as I walked Toby across I snapped off his leash and turned him loose to run with Ellie Mae on the island of dark gray rock. They ran noses down from edge to edge, plotting their quarter acre of freedom. On the island's downstream point of sand and rock they waded out belly deep and tested the current pouring through the cut. There the dogs always think about swimming to the other side, but never do. I think they would if I wasn't present to call them back. They'd be gone to Glendale.

Standing on the shoals my focus often shifts quickly from the dogs testing their freedom to the past, to how much local history happened here fifty years before Glendale was founded. The village life that was established downstream by James Bivings in 1835 seems a little human and predictable when I'm standing at the place one early historian called the most important spot in Spartanburg County.

How is a place lost in time, its importance forgotten by almost everyone around it? How does it become simply a piece of property, an entry on a tax roll? Maybe the chaos of water falling over rocks hides it. Maybe the way the trees above my head knit the sky and land together makes it difficult to see why this place might matter or why we as a community might want to save it for the future. Something keeps the upper shoals out of the public consciousness of my community, but I'm not sure just what.

I know from Manning that the ridge on the west side of the creek above the upper shoals is a subdivision waiting to happen—high, flat land adjacent to the Calhoun Lakes development. I've been told local developers have coveted the property for fifty years. The Milliken family has been a good steward, but how many years will it be before they sell it? If it's valuable as real estate today, then how much more valuable will it be in fifty years when this end of Spartanburg County "builds out," as most of the land upstream nearer the city already has?

When I stand on the old, worn rocks I don't want to think much about the time to come out here. It's too painful. I think instead about history, and it's easy to imagine when the country around me was still raw, a frontier, not yet settled by anyone.

In the late eighteenth century the early colonial settlers traveled south down the Old Georgia Road and crossed the creek. They were looking for land, not "real estate." They wanted land for growing crops and grazing livestock, and the big floodplain stretching upstream on Lawson's Fork was prime. They also needed tools, and so when an early ironworks was established on the creek, it was a source of such essentials.

The ironworks was on the south side of the creek, 125 yards downstream from a cut stone abutment of the old trolley crossing, close to where I was standing. Several old maps place it there, and a hundred years ago one old-time historian described its site precisely saying, "Until a few years ago, when the pond was raised, a part of the old mill was visible, but since that time it is wholly submerged beneath the waters."

This area of South Carolina early on was even called "The Old Iron District." The industry had begun in New England in the 1640s, but Joseph Buffington established what was probably one of the first ironworks in the state at the upper shoals in 1773. Later it became known as Wofford's Iron Works.

A successful iron operation needed a number of things that this raw territory near Lawson's Fork had in abundance—crystalline rock for building furnaces, forges, and factory buildings; abundant hardwood forests to make charcoal for smelting iron ore; marble to melt with the ore and help purify it; and a shoals for power.

"And because of it the creek's still probably not that healthy down there," David says. "We sent them a letter asking to include Augusta National as one of the courses we were sampling for amphibian diversity, but they politely declined."

I've had dreams of getting Foster, Norman, Randy, and David into a discussion about sustainable golf courses, but it just isn't happening. It's too hard to focus everyone on a golf course. Everyone wanders off to hit a shot from a different part of the fairway, and by the time we reconvene the topic's shifted to something more mundane. "We've been playing together for thirty years," Foster says, "and when I get home my wife always asks me, 'What did you talk about?' and I always say, 'Nothing.' "

They play through nine, ten, eleven, twelve. David's found his old game for a hole or two, and Norman's birdied two or three holes in a row. On thirteen Randy points out to Foster that if they want to be competitive they need to step it up now, with five holes to go. The thirteenth is a long par four running straight and flat next to Country Club Road. They all four smack it off the tee, and it amazes me that after the second shot these four old friends are all within fifty feet of the flag.

"You know there were no trees on this course until Mr. Milliken planted these pines in the 1950s," Norman says as we walk toward the green. "All these big pines are his."

This gets them all talking about trees and golf courses. "There's one woman who lets us know what she thinks about every tree we have to take down," Norman says. "Every time she sees me she complains about one near the clubhouse we took down years ago to build the patio. I say, well, you can have the tree or the patio, take your choice."

Standing on the thirteenth green Norman points out the flagstick to David. There are small "eyes" on the fat middle of the pole, "lasers that can give you exact distance to the hole in yards," Norman says. "A lot has changed since you last played."

Some for the better, Foster points out. "Can you imagine

our fathers carrying their bags like we're doing today at fifty years old?"

And I do try. It's hard for me since my father died when I was five, and I can't imagine him ever thinking about golf, much less playing it. I'm sure it would have looked like a waste of good acreage to a farm boy like him. He was from eastern North Carolina, though at the end of his life he was running a service station and selling gas to more than a few golfers on Highway 1 just south of Pinehurst.

How did I avoid the golf bug? I probably have as much right as anyone to catch it. I was born in 1954 in Moore County General Hospital right outside of Pinehurst. Strangely enough, fate would put my mother in the same room that October with maybe the greatest female athlete of all time, Babe Didrikson Zaharias. Babe was in the hospital, suffering from the cancer that would kill her two years later, and my mother told me often about how Babe held me in her strong arms and rocked me.

By 1954 the Texas tomboy's glory days were behind her— All-American women's basketball player, softball pitcher, the Olympics of 1932, and the five different American and world records she held in various track and field events. Golf had been her main interest for twenty-five years, and so she was a frequent visitor to Pinehurst. And yet it isn't until now, fifty years later, that I've even thought about golf in any serious manner. Not even the legendary David Scott was rocked in the arms of Babe Zaharias.

The next few holes go by fast as we approach the end of our morning walking the club course. Norman's still hitting it well. David's hanging in there. Foster's game has left him, and he gets so mad on fifteen that he slings an iron up the course. On the sixteenth Norman points out a spot where the hole doglegs a little to the right. "I walked the course once with Mike Dirr," he said, referring to the famous horticulturalist from the University of Georgia. "We got to this spot and I said to Dirr, 'Now, this is a very strategic tree,' pointing to an old pine. 'It's not strategic for long,' Dirr said. 'It's dead.' "

Our day on the course is drawing quickly to a close as we make the turn toward the final hole. I've enjoyed the morning, and I think everyone else has as well. In the end, I disagree with the famous remark by Mark Twain. This round of golf with four old friends was not "a good walk spoiled."

On the eighteenth the fog moves in. "Like *Bagger Vance*," Foster says, making reference to a golf film I've never seen. I watch as it eats the green behind us.

"That's unusual here," Randy says, the last of the storm leaving us this gift as the fog floats up from the creek bottom. The four friends hit their final drives uphill toward the clubhouse. They all putt out. For what it's worth, Norman wins.

"David, I hope you come back before thirty years passes again," Foster says.

David picks up his ball on the final green. "It wasn't a bad day," he says, putting it in the pocket of his baggy shorts. "I lost one ball and found three."

> The most fundamental and important truths are still to be found in the life around us, in the significant distractions of any odd moment in pasture or woodlot, river bend or forest.
>
> CHRISTOPHER CAMUTO, *Hunting from Home*

I'll Take My Stand

I've only been hunting once in my life. It was when I was fourteen, and my brother-in-law's brother Ned took me into the stark, spindly woods of southern Spartanburg County near Pacolet. This was somebody else's land, but we walked through the broken fields and woods full of rabbit tobacco and broom sedge as if we owned it. I had a borrowed .410 shotgun resting on my shoulder and red shotgun shells in my pants pockets. Squirrels and rabbits were our quarry of choice.

My brother-in-law's family worked in a cotton mill and still ate small game. We walked all morning through the cold, passing old fence posts and scraps of barbed wire sunk into trunks of trees. We climbed through the fences and stepped over red clay gullies, relics of the decades when cotton farming burnt out the topsoil. Everywhere there were clay crystal ice ridges. When stomped they quickly melted and left wet red smears on my boot soles.

We crossed the burnt brown broom sedge and watched for

rabbits. When we passed into the shadows of trees we looked up into stark blue winter sky shot through with the terminal branches of native hardwoods. It was beautiful and, being a city boy, I loved the woods as I loved nothing about the worn-out streets of the old grown-over-by-town mill village in Spartanburg where my mother and I lived.

We came up empty most of the morning. When we'd made the turn for home Ned spotted a nest high in the crook of an old oak and told me to shoot up into it. He wanted me to at least have the sense of hunting before we headed back for dinner. I'd been working my cold feet all morning to stay loose, and so hefting the gun and squeezing off a shot warmed another part of my body. I had an easy shot, straight up, and the .410 didn't kick much. Even I could hit a stationary nest the size of a globe.

The nest exploded. Twigs and leaves came floating down. In a strange surreal moment not one but two squirrels tumbled out and hit the ground, like socks filled with marbles, in front of me. Ned picked the carcasses up and stuffed one into each pocket of his old brown jacket. Dried squirrel blood lined the seams from other morning hunts. He laughed about how we'd have squirrel brains and eggs for breakfast, how his mama would make squirrel dumplings for supper "just like chicken dumplings."

When I recite my hunting story I think of the haunting scene at the conclusion of "The Bear" in Faulkner's *Go Down Moses*, when young Isaac McCaslin follows the sound of someone beating metal on metal through the big bottom and finds Boon Hogganbeck with his back against a big gum tree full of forty or fifty squirrels, "one green maelstrom of mad leaves, while from time to time, singly or in twos and threes, squirrels would dart down the trunk and whirl without stopping and rush back up again." Boon was sitting there as Isaac approached, his gun scattered about him in pieces and the old man hammering on the breach of it with the barrel, shouting at the boy who approached him, the one he had helped teach to hunt, "Get out of here! Don't touch them. Don't touch a one of them! They're mine!"

I tell this story to establish that I am not really the hunting kind, though I am susceptible to its pleasures and comforts. I'm no Isaac McCaslin or even Boon Hogganbeck, and most of the thrill I've felt for hunting comes from reading literary sources like Faulkner and Hemingway. I've never even sat in a tree stand, or stood in a duck blind, or shot a turkey and removed the chin hair to hang from the rearview mirror of my pickup, never listened to what my friend James Kilgo in *Deep Enough for Ivorybills* calls "the song fest," the ritual telling of hunting tales next to a roaring campfire after the guns fall silent.

In the intervening thirty-five years since I shot the squirrels, small game hunting has declined because the old farm fields have grown up into forests, divided into subdivisions, or become private hunt clubs. Deer and turkey have come to thrive in the rural margins of the southern piedmont, and sport hunting has become a leading recreation for the working and upper classes of the region. There are people who still hunt squirrels and rabbits, but there are surely no clubs dedicated to squirrel hunting as there are to whitetail and wild turkey. There are no squirrel songfests and probably no more Boon Hogganbecks out there with their backs to a big gum. The hunting plots near an urban area, like the one across the creek—two hundred acres of deer and turkey habitat—are getting as rare as squirrel hunters.

For these reasons I've always been intrigued with the far side of the creek. Last summer, early, we listened for days while a tractor plowed the creek bottom. We stood on our side and guessed that they were planting corn—"for the wildlife to eat."

But the other side of the creek remained unexplored territory. When we moved in, the owners made it clear that there is "at least one deer" shot over there each year, and so they didn't want us wandering their land, but we couldn't resist. We wanted at least once to walk the lay of the land on the other side of the creek. We knew it was trespassing, but one Sunday in early September before deer season kicked in, Betsy and I crossed Lawson's Fork on a big downed poplar log just downstream from where our path empties into the sewer right-of-way. The trail was muddy and slick where the creek had jumped its channel and flooded into the path two days before. There were raccoon tracks everywhere in the fresh mud. "An army of raccoons passed here," Betsy said, marveling at the number of them. "Or one very busy one," I added.

We cut our way through smilax to reach the big poplar trunk, so it felt like a fairy tale crossing. The creek was running high—red-brown and rolling along—after another all-night rain. The poplar was dead, so there were shelves of fungi growing on it, making the footing a little tricky. Three or four piles of raccoon scat crowned the ridge of the log, showing the animals had been using it as a creek crossing as well. I snapped off a couple of dead limbs that were in the way, and we headed across. Halfway, I turned and looked behind me. Betsy was scooting on her butt mostly as I high-wired it over in front of her. We reached the other shore and had to fight through more greenbrier and privet to make landfall.

We looked around when we were firmly on the other side. Over there the creek is bordered by privet, cottonwood, small maples, and box elder, just like on our side, but flood debris is everywhere, deposited by the slower water of the big bend as the creek makes a turn in front of our place—plastic buckets, soft drink bottles, balls, even a notebook for some sort of corporate training, anything that floats. The soil is dark and alluvial on the other side, but there's a big sandbar right where the creek turns.

Stepping out of the border of trees along the creek the field

opens up too—ten acres of planted bottom with the big transmission towers right through the middle of it all. We walked out
into the sun and acres of light—perfect soil and open territory
for growing things, which this patch of bottom has probably
been doing for thousands of years.

Betsy looked down and asked what was growing at her feet,
so I pulled up a small turnip, wiped it on my shirt, and took
a bite. It tasted like a radish—a little bit peppery. Betsy took a
little bite too.

Turnips were a much more common southern food a generation ago. My 1943 *Joy of Cooking* has nine turnip recipes, various
ways of mashing and baking. I turned the root in my hand. The
same genus as mustard and cabbage, it's an import, a native of
Europe. The primary root is nutritious but also used as stock
feed. The flowers are yellow.

Rape is the old generic term for turnip, and there are white
turnips (what our neighbor has planted in his field) and yellow turnips, known as rutabagas. In Irish mythology there's a
character called Stingy Jack who tricked the devil and wasn't
allowed to enter either heaven or hell. Stingy Jack roamed the
earth holding a glowing coal in a hollow turnip, so the turnip
lantern became the festival light for Halloween and also the ancient symbol of a "damned soul." The English and Irish carved
faces into turnips to scare Jack and other spirits away.

It's said if you cut up a turnip, rub a wart with it, then bury
the turnip, the wart will disappear, but neither of us had any
warts, and there was no time to try this trick in that bottomland
field. "Turnip greens, turnip greens, / Good old turnip greens.
/ Corn bread and buttermilk, / And good old turnip greens,"
a folk song goes.

We walked deeper into the sunlit turnip field, and Betsy
pulled up a very big one quite easily. She wanted to carry it
back to Russell for "show and tell" at school. It was ten inches
around and had a pink bottom and small root. The greens were

stunted, but I snipped off a piece of the toothed leaves and ate some of that too. It had that same peppery taste of the root. Who eats turnips now? It was somehow comforting to think of turnips growing in a field across our creek.

But this was no agricultural field trip. We were explorers, so off we went. To our west, on the edge of the field, we could see a metal tripod deer stand covered with a camo tarp. This stand was one our neighbors use to shoot their "big deer" every year. It looked like a guard tower. In the approaching October I imagined them driving down the hill in their pickups before dawn, parking on the ridge, walking out and climbing up into the stand. I thought of them sitting hours up there, watching the deer move through the turnip field until the right big buck finally wandered into sight, a buck they'd seen signs of for months, one that had most likely crossed the creek and drifted through our very backyard nibbling flowers at dawn or dusk. And then KAPOW, one shot, and it would be over for that wild deer.

There was something magical about the spot for me. The hunters had done a good job of placing the stand. It had clear coverage of the field, and from the little rise it sat on, you could even see a section of the creek. Deer tracks were everywhere, around it on all sides. Local landowners who are lucky enough to find themselves at the beginning of the twenty-first century owning the ancient bottoms are really the salvation of the rest of us, since the little choices these blessed landowners make now—sometimes not always conscious or conservation decisions—are really the difference between losing it all for the next generation and keeping many of the most important parts of the piedmont healthy.

Looking back across the creek at our high ridge I felt time slip a little, and I could see back past human settlement to the Archaic period wanderers who camped next to our house site and how they looked out over this field from there to where we were standing, the bottom maybe kept clear of undergrowth by the fires they set. Maybe it was all river cane over here. It was surely all one piece back then, not divided up into "our" land and somebody else's land. I looked up once more at the deer stand. I felt a pang of guilt for trespassing on my neighbor's property, but knew I had no plans to ever come back.

Why didn't I hunt? Maybe if I hunted, my neighbors would invite me over, and I could make contact with this place in the way they do. I could see their land through their eyes. One reason I don't hunt is that I don't much like guns, and I definitely don't like loud noises.

But that's not it really. I don't hunt because I don't like to kill things, even though I know creation spins along on the dance of "tooth and claw." I never blew up frogs with firecrackers as a kid, never stomped anthills or scorched tent caterpillars with kerosene, never put salt on slugs to watch them shrivel. I never lobbied for a BB gun to knock off songbirds.

When I think about hunting I always think of Faulkner's stories, but I also always think of James Kilgo. Kilgo was a longtime University of Georgia professor, novelist, and essayist. Before he died Jim was one of the most compelling voices in southern literature for understanding the southerner's "outdoor heritage." He was from the low country of South Carolina, the watershed of the Great Pee Dee, but he had roots in the upstate as well. He knew what it meant to have red clay on his boots. He understood the rituals of hunting deer as a valuable access door into the world of community, family, and the history of the rural South. He walked back through that door and found that it led not only to hunting but also to literature.

As a child Jim says that he was "enthralled" by nature. When he was in the woods he reports he had "no past and the future held no threat." He also reports a car trip through a lowcountry South Carolina swamp that was a "deep place, deep enough for ivorybills, with no far side to come out on."

I became friends with Kilgo late in his life, but by the time we were close he never talked of hunting. He had mostly abandoned his beloved Groton Plantation hunt club and found his inspiration in family, fishing, his church, his friends, and conservation, except for one big-game expedition to Africa that became his last book, *Colors of Africa.*

Almost all I know of hunting I learned from Kilgo's essays in *Deep Enough for Ivorybills* and *Inheritance of Horses,* or the books he loved and recommended such as Christopher Camuto's *Hunting from Home,* Franklin Burroughs's *Billy Watson's Croker Sack,* or Richard Nelson's *Heart and Blood,* a study of white-tailed deer in America.

Jim never saw our house. He was already sick by the time we bought our lots here. He would have loved the creek bottom—not quite "deep enough for ivorybills"—but at least deep enough so that the deer and turkey and songbirds moved up and down Lawson's Fork with ease.

After Kilgo was diagnosed with cancer he gave up hunting for ten years. He said before he died that he did not need to shoot a deer to survive, but he also claimed that he wasn't totally happy with the loss. "Giving up hunting," he says, "was merely indicative of a larger resignation." I guess by this Kilgo meant resignation to death.

Jim Kilgo found his years without hunting full of a "sense of wonder," but for him much more of his fulfillment came through reading beautiful writing and following clear thinking about the human/natural world relationship.

The conversation about nature writing was another powerful "songfest," one of a different sort, and he participated in it fully at conferences and in discussions with friends he had made through the writing life. In his final ten years Jim Kilgo was able to survey a line along the border of nature writing and outdoor writing as few others have. He joined Rick Bass, Jim Harrison, Thomas McGuane, and others as apologists for "the hunting life," and he did it beautifully. How could I not think of Kilgo while standing in my neighbor's private hunting preserve?

Let the hunters have at it. Let them scale their bark-biters, climbers, lock-ons, tripods, ladders, and climbing sticks all over the state and bear down with bow, muzzle-loader, or rifle. Let them indulge their "antlerless hunting season," and their "doe days," and let them bring back their tenderloins and strip off their shank roasts and grind them into venison hash.

Another reason I don't hunt is sometimes I feel more empathy for the deer than I do the humans hunting them. I'd call it kinship. Maybe I'm of the Clan of the White Tail. Like me the deer is an "edge" animal, preferring the margins to the center of things, nibbling the edges, moving under cover in small bands. They say the South Carolina whitetails are one of the purest strains of native deer in the Southeast. I like to think that when Tommy takes a deer off this property each year his hunt is tied by blood all the way back to the Pleistocene.

The shadow of the rural South that Kilgo loved was not far in the background that day when I walked across the creek with Betsy. There was a little farming going on, but rural historian Jack Temple Kirby says that if your idea of rural is family-run agriculture, your idea is a memorial to something that no longer exists. Most of the farming done in the South today is not like this turnip and cornfield. It's big business—tree plantations, soybeans, and turf farms for the most part.

What is the rural South today if it's not agricultural? What use are all those empty acres out there along the interstates? Maybe from the point of view of most southerners "the new rural landscape" is mostly about recreation, freedom, and escape—deer hunting, four-wheeling, hiking, all the things that go on behind our house. The fourth growth woodlots covering much of the "rural" piedmont are where people often go on weekends for these activities.

As we walked I thought of a student of mine who once made a distinction between land owned by "people you know" and land owned by "rich people, government, or corporations." Land owned by people you know is treated differently, more respectfully, than other land. The large tracts with abstract ownership are where the teenage "recreation" takes place—mudding, bonfires, and general rowdiness.

Suburban teenagers, like the ones we have to deal with, often see land vacant of human occupation as a sort of "commons," just as their ancestors once did as well. Instead of running pigs and cows to fatten them in the common fields and woods, the youth of the South let themselves run wild in these open spaces.

The idea of a rural commons has always offered an interesting contrast to the idea of "property rights" in the South. Kirby says the idea of a commons survived in the South longer than in other regions. Individual property rights is one of the values conservative southerners hold so dearly, yet the idea of land held in common for the use of the whole community is an idea probably even older. Another student once told me the story of his family's struggle with their neighbor on seventy acres in rural South Carolina. They discovered the neighbor had built several tree stands on their property. When they confronted him, they suggested he simply ask permission if he wanted to hunt their land. Then they asked him to remove the stands. They came back the next fall and the stands were gone. Instead of encroaching on his neighbor's property the good old boy had simply rebuilt the stands on the edge of his own one-acre wooded lot—facing toward his neighbor's larger parcel.

Before we abandoned our neighbor's land for our own and returned to our anxious dogs, Betsy sat for a few minutes on top of a mound of dirt and debris directly across the creek from our trail. She said she liked the view of our house from over there. It looked different from that side of the creek, even more like a sailing ship.

But sailing into what? I thought of Jim Kilgo again and how different the worlds we'd staked out had become. He divided his world clearly between "hearth" and "field." What Kilgo refers to as hearth consists of his domestic life: suburbia, church, and family. He says in his writing that his "truest joy" is the time he spent in the field in the company of sportsmen. There was no division here for me. The field for me is right out my back door.

We made our way back down to the log and over to our place. It had been the briefest of visits, but I told myself it would have to do. I wouldn't go back over and violate my neighbor's trust or ever risk stepping into his line of fire. After all, if I am from the Clan of the White Tail, I could be mistaken for one. All we brought back was the one turnip and an altered perspective, seeing our house sailing through the forests above us. Our hounds greeted us from high on the deck as we approached, barking to show they were glad we were home.

We could see our beagle Toby pacing back and forth, tail held straight up at attention. We looked up at our chubby dog. We knew he'd gladly trade the security of kibble and sleeping on his couch for just one run at a wild deer in the creek bottom.

Dogs are us, only innocent.

CYNTHIA HEIMEL

Bottom Dog

Within a week of moving in we saw a funny little orange beagle
hunting on the bottomland trail below our house. The floodplain was the beagle's territory. He divided up the hillsides
and worked the scents he found for deer. Toby and Ellie Mae
formed a chorus of similar sounds every time I got up my nerve
and let our dogs off leash to run in the privet.

The beagle didn't live in the bottom—he had a home up the
street, in a brick split-level ranch house on the corner. He lived
like dogs used to in the country and the suburbs before the
county had leash laws and concerned owners installed electric
fences. He slept in a plastic igloo in the garage, had two stain-
less steel bowls (one for water and one for kibble), and several
toys scattered in the driveway. I don't think he ever went inside.
Nobody had to cut his toenails. They were worn down from
ranging all over the tar and gravel roads of the neighborhood.
The beagle had an admirable—if risky—freedom.

When we first arrived, the sound of the beagle hunting was

constant, a sharp series of barks that continued for hours sometimes. Our first year in the house the beagle's song was our sound track, the dark trees out my windows his vast stage.

Right away I gave the beagle deep metaphoric significance, much more than he deserved. He became my way of making contact with one aspect of the past of this place. He was a hunting dog caught—like us—on the edge of these foreign domestic suburbs.

The early Indians had hunting dogs here in the watershed of Lawson's Fork. I imagined that in the baying of the beagle I could hear all the way back to De Soto or even further, into the paleo past, when the first small hunting bands ranged up the Broad River basin hunting for bison and mastodon.

Dogs were more than tools for the people who lived here thousands of years before us. Humans and dogs in North America have a relationship going back twelve thousand years. Cave paintings show dogs walking with early humans, much as they still walk with us today. Dogs back then occupied a similar favored status as our two hounds. They carried gear, hunted, and guarded the camps. At night they curled close around the feet of the foragers who had walked long distances that day. They sought the warmth of human fires just as our hounds curl close to our hearth now.

But Toby and Ellie Mae are no longer tools, or if they are tools their use is mostly as companions. Sometimes our dogs even feel like family. Because of this complex relationship I often treat our dogs more like children. I fear for their safety the moment they step out the front door unleashed. I monitor what they eat, and I rush them to the doctor if they show signs of illness. The lives of our dogs are lived in stark contrast to the roaming of our neighbor's beagle hound.

Seven years ago, when Toby was little more than a puppy, Betsy lived in Converse Heights downtown. She called him "the Marco Polo of beagles" because of his frequent escapes and explorations. Once Toby was found on the second floor of a house under construction four blocks away. Another time he escaped the fence and turned up four streets away in the other direction, scavenging for scraps left from another contractor's lunch sack.

When we moved out here, Ellie Mae was too old to disappear into the privet and boggy depths of the creek bottom, so we let her walk with us unleashed. We figured at fourteen she'd earned some freedom. She'd wander out into the woods a little ways but always returned. Life on the edge of the suburbs suited her. She doesn't get along with any dog except Toby, and she was always nervous when the wandering beagle hound was around. "Would Toby be that color if we let him run in the swamp?" Betsy asked once as we watched Toby and the mud-stained beagle playing in the street.

Life for a backyard dog is confining, so when Ellie Mae was much younger I'd meet a friend with his three dogs on Sundays and we'd turn them loose in nine-thousand-acre Croft State Park in the southern part of the county. He had Sam, a golden retriever, Feah, a three-legged mutt, and a medium hound-mix named Otis.

We'd bushwhack along Kelsey Creek. We could hear the hound voices of Ellie Mae and Otis out ahead baying at some game trail. We imagined the other two right behind, all four noses following some mysterious map we could not reproduce with trails. We trusted they would return, and they always did but once.

One Sunday Otis went out into the woods, but he did not come back with the other dogs. It took an extra hour to get that hound back. "Otis came back when he was ready, which was never," Gerald says when he remembers that Sunday running the dogs. "I was annoyed, but mostly embarrassed."

On the morning Otis died he could barely get off his bed, but the old hound slipped out of the fence anyway and disappeared for hours into the city park next to their neighborhood. "That damn dog staggered to his feet and disappeared one more time," Gerald said. "Otis did what he wanted."

Our first months here we listened as the beagle hound worked the bottom for scent trails all night. When we drove past we saw that he slept all day in the street or under a crape myrtle beside the split-level. Afternoons, when Betsy and I walked our two hounds down to the beagle's corner he'd wake up, easy in his freedom. He seemed to like Toby best, and they would play when I dropped Toby's leash.

In October a hand-lettered "for sale" sign appeared at the beagle's house, and we knew that when the couple moved we'd lose their dog as well. It never occurred to me that the hound might leave before the people did, either given away, taken to the pound, lost, or shot as he hunted endlessly in the bottom.

We'd gotten to know the hound, but we didn't know the people who owned him. We've met other neighbors, and they'd told us the couple—the beagle hound's humans—had been through a divorce and the dog may have been caught in the crossfire, left pretty much on his own. One neighbor reported the hound grew more and more independent in the months since the husband left.

Then one day I noticed I had not heard him hunting. Had it been a day? A week? The sound of the hound baying in the bottom had become such a backdrop to my days, but somehow he had disappeared without us noticing.

I wanted to know what happened to the beagle, but I was reluctant to go up and ask the wife, who was still living at the house. After all, he was her dog. What business was it of mine? Now when we walked to the corner the neighborhood seemed destitute, tame, lacking some essential sound, some deep wildness, the baying of the beagle hound, and the absence of what we had come to call "the bottom dog."

Then one morning Toby and Ellie Mae sat bolt upright and

jumped down off the sofa. They started barking and we couldn't get them to stop. They were both pacing at the door. We let them out on the deck overlooking the floodplain, and then we heard what they had heard—dogs barking down on the creek. Was it the beagle hound returned?

I left Betsy and our house hounds on the deck and went down to the creek to investigate. I could tell the dogs were barking just upstream from a big cottonwood fallen across the creek in the last flood. I couldn't get close enough to see clearly what was going on, so I went back to get binoculars. When I returned I found a good angle and saw a huge tan buck standing in the middle of the creek. Two stray dogs, one a gaunt ruddy shepherd mix and the other a pit bull, were on the edge of the water, tag-team barking at the deer.

The buck held his ground but looked tired, as if he'd been holding the dogs off for quite awhile. He lunged at them with his rack every time they tried to approach. It seemed like something you might see in the Alaskan backcountry or on *Animal Planet*, but this was not the Brooks Range. This was three miles from Morgan Square in downtown Spartanburg.

I ran back to get Betsy. We worked our way upstream just above the unfolding drama. We broke through the underbrush for a view. The dogs hopped around in the water, and the buck shifted to keep his rack between his body and the dogs.

When the huge buck looked up I saw that it was an eight-pointer. He also had a massive, round, dark growth on the end of the right trailing tine. It was like a burl, but made of bone, not wood. The burl was so big—the size of a volley ball—that I thought at first the defensive buck had speared one of the many loose balls on Lawson's Fork and caught it on his antler. The growth was some bone abnormality that made the buck look surreal.

We were so close that we could look down from the bank directly into his eyes. Then the buck looked up and saw us, and I could see fear, but also calculation, like he was thinking, "OK, now there are humans to deal with. What's more of a threat, these two crazy stray dogs or these people?"

As the deer considered the risk of bolting in either direction I thought of that Robert Frost poem "The Most of It" where the speaker is standing on the shore of a lake. He's alone. He's thinking all he's going to get when he throws his voice across the lake is an echo off the cliff on the far side. Instead a huge buck surprises him, and it "crashed in the cliff's talus on the other side" and swam the lake, coming ashore "pouring like a waterfall" right in front of him "and stumbled through the rocks with horny tread, / And forced the underbrush." Our morning had been like that. In a couple of seconds the real buck decided we were more of a threat and disappeared into the fringe of summer woods across from us.

The two crazy strays looked up at me as if they remembered something, paused for a moment, then wheeled in the shallows and took off chasing the buck downstream. From the deck we heard our own dogs answer the barks of the dogs hot in pursuit of the deer. If Toby and Ellie Mae had their way there would be four dogs instead of two in the hunt.

I came home and called my neighbor who hunts the land and told him about the dogs running the deer. He said, "The one with the growth? That's a shooter." He'd been watching the eight point buck for two years and planned to take it soon. "You know what I'd do," he said, and I knew it wasn't good news for the strays.

I related the conversation to Betsy when I got off the phone. "He meant he'd shoot the dogs," I said.

"Shoot the dogs?"

"Shoot the dogs before they kill the deer he wants to kill later."

We didn't own a gun, and it was the kind of choice we were glad we didn't have to make. It's not that we're completely naive about such situations. We both know what wildness can do to those once tame, but neither of us wanted to think about what it meant to hear those desperate hungry strays in the creek bottom: dogs run deer in hopes of killing and even eating them. It wasn't a game we'd observed in our backyard, and it wasn't the grand score of some wilderness symphony either.

All morning we talked about the wild dogs in the bottom. The Romantic in me wanted their freedom from domesticity to draw them closer to their ancient wolf cousins, but to our neighbor they were really not much better than a couple of convicts escaped and on a killing spree, and he wasn't opposed to the death penalty. We talked about instincts, freedom, and free will.

That afternoon we walked Toby and Ellie Mae up Mustang Drive instead of down the hill in the direction of the house where the bottom dog had lived. We talked about how much we missed him and how the scene with dogs reminded us of how uncertain his life was hunting the bottom.

I looked down at our beagle and felt guilty. After all, a dog's a dog and needs to run a little. I let Toby off the leash to hunt the margins of our subdivision street with Ellie Mae. Though I tried to keep my eye on him, he disappeared for a few minutes, and then I spotted him ahead of us up on the small scrubby hill that Taurus Circle swings around. Worried he would disappear into the deep woods I went up to snap him back on the leash. When I approached I saw his tail rotating high and fast, a beagle's sign that it's on to something.

When I called, Toby turned, and I saw four baby rabbits filling his mouth. One was hanging by its back end. Another had its tiny head protruding from the dog's mouth.

"Toby," I said. "You drop those rabbits." But this was finally a moment of free will for Toby. Maybe it was worth all those hours on the other end of a leash. He chomped three times and swallowed.

If you clear a forest you'd better pray continuously. . . . God doesn't like a clear cut. It makes his heart turn cold, makes him wince and wonder what went wrong with his creation.

JANISSE RAY, *Ecology of a Cracker Childhood*

The Unnatural History
of a Clear-cut

On a Tuesday in August I drove to town, as I often do, along Lake Forest Drive. Just before I crossed the creek I noticed a bulldozer sitting close to the road on the large parcel of bottomland on the east side. I slowed down and saw where the big cat had pushed several trees out of the way, beginning to open what could have been a road into the bottom.

That morning the bottomland forest off Lake Forest Drive looked deep and mysterious, like something straight out of Faulkner's "The Bear"—"sombre, impenetrable." We've seen deer, beaver, turkey, gray fox, possum, raccoon crossing the road there.

I drove on to town, but I was already concerned. By the time I returned two hours later and saw the bulldozer still sitting there I was panicked. The bulldozer was only a quarter-mile upstream from our house on our side of the creek. It may have been idle, but it was hard at work in my imagination. Since we built our house, Lake Forest Drive has served as a line of first defense against the development upstream on the Lawson's Fork. As long as the large parcels of floodplain stayed wooded and raw I always felt safe downstream. The south side of the bridge was where the yards ended. It was where space ceased being divided easily into real estate. I knew the property was owned, but in my mind it seemed secure simply by its wild presence and the fact that once or twice a year, when Lawson's Fork climbs out of its banks, five or six feet of water flows through it. I drove past and extrapolated outward from the bulldozer's single swatch. I could see the whole floodplain opened up and planted with grass. I knew I even preferred the kudzu encroaching from the road to the anticipated clarity of the bulldozer's clearance.

In 1973 the Country Club of Spartanburg had bought the parcel of floodplain from the Pierce family, saying they wanted to expand the golf course to the other side of the creek. At that time the land had been farmed for roughly two hundred years and was clear of timber, crisscrossed with dirt farm roads. Later the club purchased a smaller parcel on the west side of the creek.

For thirty years the country club did nothing with its property on the east and west sides of the creek. Timber returned. A mixed hardwood bottomland forest covered the tract, and it gained some maturity, though we'd heard discussions were ongoing on the country club board as to the best "use" of the land.

The original golf course idea had been scrubbed because flooding was a concern. Over the years, propositions had surfaced and disappeared: a skeet-shooting range, an equestrian center, and most recently a "golf practice facility." In the last decade SPACE, the local land trust, began to approach the board about conservation uses of the land to protect the creek and woods, but they couldn't even get on the meeting agendas.

I made some notes in my journal about the bulldozer when

I arrived home. I belonged to SPACE's land committee, and we had a meeting the next day at a local restaurant. When everybody was settled in, I asked about the road and the bulldozer's arrival on Lake Forest Drive. Probably just a kudzu removal project, someone said. Or something to do with sewer-line work, another offered. Several of them said that they, being club members, would know if there were plans to clear-cut the property.

The next day, driving into town on Thursday morning, Betsy called on the cell phone to report that more heavy equipment had arrived. After the phone call I was angry and went straight to my study and hammered out an e-mail to several of the SPACE land committee members. Something was going on down at the club property and we'd better get on it.

One committee member must have been online because a response came straight back. She had heard there had already been an encounter between an angry Lake Forest Drive neighbor and the loggers. I drove by once or twice during the day, and it seemed they were going to start with the smaller parcel, so maybe there was still hope of stopping them before the big clear-cut started.

Friday morning I drank coffee and paced up and down on the deck. I could hear the chainsaws in the distance. They sounded mournful, like dogs howling.

I phoned a country club board member I knew. He heard me out and admitted a clear-cut was underway and that the plan, as he understood it, was to "clear the property on both sides of the creek and then look at it without trees and decide whether to put in a golf practice facility or not."

"So it's a speculative clear-cut," I said, angry at the prospect. "Purely cash motivated if you don't go forward with the facility."

"That's how I understand it," he said.

"That timber's worth about as much as one SUV in the club's front parking lot."

Betsy was standing on the deck, and she too could hear the

saws in the distance. I could see the anger rising in her face. "Ask him if they've talked to SPACE?" Betsy whispered.

"There's been a logging company interested for some time in the timber," he said. "It's a lot less money than an SUV."

Then he brought up beavers backing up a creek on the property, how the club needed to "protect their investment" and not let beavers take it away. I asked him if anyone on the board had ever considered this piece of property as a valuable wildlife habitat, as a potential green space so close to the urban core and seen the beavers as part of that?

"Not to my knowledge."

I asked about stream buffers.

"We've talked about it," he said. The loggers had agreed to leave aesthetic buffers along the road and a strip along the stream. But he had no idea exactly how wide or whether the buffers were actually written into the contract.

Newly passed city ordinances call for hundred-foot buffers along Lawson's Fork, but he reminded me that the club property is outside the city and that riparian buffers mean nothing in the county.

Had club membership been informed about the plan?

"No, the board feels it's our call," he said. They believed the membership would agree with their decision, but then he paused and conceded that they may have underestimated the concern: "Yesterday the board chairman's phone was ringing off the hook all day."

Betsy stood at the railing and listened to the chainsaws and to my side of the conversation. When I finished the call she was furious.

"Well, there's no doubt about it—it's a clear-cut," I said.

"We've got to stop it," she said and grabbed the phone from me. She called the country club and talked with the club manager. After a frustrating three minute conversation she slammed the phone down and walked away.

"What did he say?" I asked.

"He said it's their property and they can do whatever they please with it," she said, slumped on the couch.

"The club manager's right," I said, trying to be logical, to see both sides of the issue. "But this is much more than a simple property rights question."

"Right! It's a wetlands, an important one. The club's own membership has brought up saving that property," Betsy said. "The board would never discuss it. In my mind that's a failure of responsibility and has little to do with rights."

The logging picked up in intensity over the weekend on the west side of creek. We called Mary Walter, the executive director of SPACE, but she was out of town. I sent e-mails to SPACE board members, and talk began with neighbors on Lake Forest Drive. The first photos of the clear-cut began to circulate on the Internet.

On Sunday morning the board member I'd talked with called back to say that the club president was out of town on a fishing trip. He was not returning calls. The president was the only one who could stop what was happening. First thing Monday he would check on the streamside buffers.

That afternoon Betsy called a club member living next to the clear-cut, and the two of them began plotting what could be done to stop the logging. They talked of making signs for a Monday morning protest. They planned to meet at 8 a.m. and take action against the loggers.

"What are you going to do?" I asked.

"We're going to stop it—now, and for good."

We sat on the deck and talked about it all. I was paralyzed and felt a little hopeless. I didn't want to go with Betsy to protest the clear-cut because I wanted to write about it in my weekly column. Betsy said she was hopeful, that she had faith in the community. "Once the club membership knows what's really happening they'll rally around the trees and the creek," she predicted.

I loved my wife's spirit and hopeful optimism about it all, though I was more cynical and told her so: "The board of the club can do anything they want with the club. They only have to ask the membership for approval of one thing—raising membership fees. Everything else about the management of the club is settled by the board alone."

Betsy drove to Wal-Mart late in the evening and purchased poster board and colored markers, and sat on the dining room floor cross-legged like a kid with a science project, making her flimsy, colorful signs—"Save Lawson's Fork" and "Save our Wetlands," and "This is a Wildlife Corridor" and "Senseless Destruction."

On Monday morning I sat at home and worked the phones, trying to get in touch with the key SPACE players. Betsy went off to the clear-cut.

When she arrived a few others were already there, and the logging had stopped. Earlier in the morning the woman who lived next door had simply walked into the clear-cut while the skidders were piling the newly cut logs up and told the perplexed loggers to stop cutting. Being polite southerners, the loggers did what the lady told them.

Betsy and four others formed a picket line on Lake Forest Drive and handed out fliers denouncing the clear-cut to passing cars. The loggers sat behind them on their skidders and dozers, and waited for the club forester to arrive. One TV station came out, and two local newspaper reporters took notes for stories.

When the club's forester drove up, he was hopping mad. He walked up to the line of protesters and played the trespassing card first: "This is club property. You need to leave."

The woman who'd silenced the dozers shot back, "I'm a member of the club. I think that makes it my property. I'm staying."

The forester saw quickly that things were a little more complicated than he had planned and tried to reason with the five protesters. He argued this wasn't a wetland, that there's nothing wrong with clear-cutting, that it's an age-old forestry technique and actually the best way to clear the parcel. After nothing worked, the forester used his cell to call in reinforcements.

The club president arrived a few minutes later, back from his fishing trip, and things really heated up. The protesters and the club president yelled at each other, skirmishing back and forth, Betsy related to me after she returned.

This was like something she'd read about other places, not on the lower east side of Spartanburg. The president held his position, using the beavers for cover. The beavers were stinking up the neighborhood by damming the creek, he had argued. The beavers were destroying their timber. Couldn't they simply understand it was an economic decision, that there was money to be lost if they didn't stop the beavers now?

"He's an accountant," I said. "What does he know about beavers?"

"This went on for fifteen minutes," Betsy said, describing the altercation. "He tried the property rights argument and the beaver argument again and again. He didn't back down, but neither did we."

She was happy, feeling empowered. The president had had it, and agreed to send the loggers home for the day if the protesters would leave the property and go home too.

At lunch Betsy and I ran into a country club member who was also a prominent member of SPACE. He'd received a cell message saying a meeting had been set up between the country club board and SPACE at 5 p.m. What was the best we could hope for? I asked.

"The ideal solution, of course, is for the country club to terminate the logging contract and preserve the entire property with a donated conservation easement," he said. "If they are not willing to do that, maybe all of us could work together, raise some money, purchase the easement, including timber rights, and reimburse the loggers for their expenses and lost profits."

It sounded reasonable, and we hoped it would work. Peyton Howell, SPACE's board president, a club member but also a passionate environmentalist, came to meet with us that afternoon at our house to plot strategy. We walked down by the creek and talked about stupidity of this action and how it could have easily been avoided. Peyton agreed that a compromise for a buffer would be no real victory.

At 5 p.m. the summit took place downtown. Soon after the meeting broke up Peyton called. The club officers had showed up with the forester and the disgruntled, out-of-work-for-the-moment loggers in tow. The SPACE representatives had arrived with aerial photos. They had spread the high-resolution photos of the property on the table to make their case about the exaggerated limits of the beaver activity. SPACE had argued there was no threat from beavers, and the other side had argued there was. It was a little like Bush and his weapons of mass destruction. Instead of chemicals, the country club had beavers.

Then the forester had seen an opening and pulled out a set of more recent photos of the territory the insurgent beavers had inundated.

SPACE then used its trump card: they offered to raise money to stop logging operation. Not interested, the board members had said. Then one bristly club board member had pulled out the property rights argument again: He said that everyone at the table needed to remember only one thing, "that the property in question belongs to us and we are doing nothing illegal. Even a buffer along the creek is something we do not, by law, have to do."

After an hour and a half the only concession the club representatives had agreed to was to leave a forty-foot buffer along the creek and next to Lake Forest Drive. SPACE had agreed they would not be involved in any further protest of the club's actions.

We sat that night and watched the local news and saw a short clip about the protests. Betsy was disheartened so few had turned out but was hopeful that the reporter had focused on the clash between the club and its own membership. She still believed that all the good people with country club memberships would understand the seriousness of the issue and come to the defense of woodland on Lawson's Fork.

And what about those beavers? Was what the accountant saying about them correct? They can be destructive and get in the way of what people want, but it was obvious to us that the beaver issue was simply formulated to deflect the attention away from the real issue—the club's lack of conservation vision. When the board looked at nearly a hundred acres of piedmont bottomland they saw property and not habitat, green space.

I'll admit that I tend to side with the beavers over the accountants. Those rodents have made a pretty remarkable recovery in South Carolina considering how at the end of the nineteenth century there were no beavers left in the eastern United States.

They were trapped out, mostly for fashion purposes, their pelts pressed into wool cloth for hats and such. After being reestablished in South Carolina a few decades ago, they've gone from absent to downright common. The animals themselves are hard to spot since they are shy and nocturnal, but anyone with an eye for beaver activity—beaver dams, gnawed saplings and adult trees near streams, drag marks on the banks of rivers and streams—can spot them almost everywhere in South Carolina, from city edges to the suburbs to the state parks.

Bring beavers up with even sensible friends and neighbors, and an argument will often ensue. Most people who have become aware of beavers are divided into two minds—those that hate them, consider them vermin to be eradicated or at least sharply controlled, and those who see their return as a sign of wildness recovered. The beaver haters see North America's largest rodent as endangering valuable bottomland timber and crops, flooding backyards, creating wet areas that were long dry.

The beaver lovers see the animals as merely recolonizing the floodplain territories we took from them for agriculture, ill-suited housing, golf courses, and roadbeds. Give them some time, the beaver lovers say, and the piedmont landscapes near streams will look like they did three hundred years ago. Leave the beavers to their natural habits and habitats, the beaver lovers would say. Some sort of balance will be recovered we haven't seen since the Scots-Irish hordes spread into the piedmont. Besides, the woodpeckers will have some grand snags to hunt for insects in the meantime.

I'm of both minds. I understand that the solutions are not as simple as many would like them to be. Property rights are property rights. Even the beavers are slaves to the state that controls them through game and wildlife laws, and somebody owns all the land they have recolonized.

I was once on a walk with South Carolina Educational Television's *NatureScene* naturalist Rudy Mancke, and I asked him about beavers. He laughed and said people dislike beavers because they are probably the animal most like human beings. They are one of the few wild animals capable of significantly altering a habitat to suit their needs.

On Tuesday morning the front page of the paper ran the story above the fold—"Standoff at the Country Club: Protesters prevent—at least for a day—eighty-five acres of forest from being clear cut."

A picture appeared showing five protesters standing in the midst of the clear-cut holding their signs, the bulldozers silent behind them. In the distance the spindly bottomland hardwoods awaited the chainsaws. Betsy has on shorts and Tevas and wears a broad-brimmed hat. She stands off to the right and holds her "Senseless Destruction" sign higher than everyone else.

I read the story, and I said to Betsy that our only victory so far was moral. "How long had it been since an issue involving land use had made the front page of the Spartanburg paper?" Many who read the story would hear about issues they'd never heard raised in our community before—riparian buffers, runoff, floodplain development, comprehensive plans for development of remaining urban forest cover.

For Betsy a moral victory wasn't nearly enough. Something had changed in Betsy since we moved to the creek. Her allegiances had shifted. A former business editor for the local paper, Betsy had never looked at development issues as only bottom-line decisions that either suit human beings or not. She was now thinking more and more "green," sometimes even more than I was. This was one of those occasions. She wanted to stop the clear-cut and wouldn't be happy until the trees were left standing on the property upstream from us. I knew it was less and less likely, but she still held out hope.

That afternoon the club met with SPACE again. The two organizations agreed to let the clear-cut proceed with a hundred-foot buffer left along both Lawson's Fork and Lake Forest Drive. They also agreed to a joint release describing the compromise and to lay the issue to rest. The release went out to the public and a letter went out to the country club membership describing the board's action, leaning heavily on the beavers.

We weren't settled though. We weren't satisfied with the compromises. They left the loggers on the land. We were disappointed in our friends at the club, and we felt that the members should have been more concerned with this significant parcel of east-side land.

That next evening Betsy walked downstream with the dogs on the trail that went through the Pierce property, past the sewer treatment plant and on upstream into the country club's prop-

erty. When she left she said she wanted to see it one final time as a forest before the saws took it all down. When she came back she marveled once again at how deep the woods were up there. She mourned for the loss to come and the ignorance that had caused it.

I don't know where loss of place falls on the sadness scale, but I know for southerners it's way above loss of money and well below loss of a loved one. We both felt a deep sadness the day the logging started back and the hardwood logs were piled higher and higher before they were hauled to the chip mill.

Over the next few weeks many club members came up to us and said the whole thing had been handled badly, but that there was little that could be done. It was a hundred-year-old institution with a set way of governing. A few made the decisions, and the others followed. That was that.

Why couldn't we leave it behind us? The club board wasn't thinking about the bigger conservation picture in our region, or what might be appropriate land use practices in the floodplain along Lawson's Fork, or how wrong it might be so late in the conservation game for the only stakeholders in this complex land-use issue to be a few men in a board room at the time of the vote. Why hadn't they asked their own membership what they should do with this large remnant of east-side wildness? The message from the beginning was that board knows best.

How did it happen that they'd discussed everything about their floodplain property but protecting it? It seemed they'd decided they would worry about the consequences later. They had a notion that they might want a driving range across the creek from their golf course. Maybe they'll do this. Maybe they won't. All the board seemed dead certain about was the clear-cut.

How did it happen that so many with so much power missed all this? That was the question that perplexed Betsy and me after the deal was cut. Many of the same people who wrote checks in support of conservation were also the members of the club now destroying wetlands and woodlands.

Still smarting from the clear-cut, I remembered that evening several years before when we had sneaked away from the party at the country club. That night we heard anthropologist Paige West speak about her work at the Crater Mountain Wildlife Management Area in Papua New Guinea that resulted in her book *Conservation Is Our Government Now*. Crater Mountain is a place where the native Gimi people live in the midst of wild country, and in the book Paige shows how even in wild country on the other side of the world ideas about space, environment, and society are socially produced. Even the Gimi tribesmen have to constantly rethink changing relationships between their environment and the forces around them.

Now I understand what Paige is saying with her title—that issues of conservation are too important today to dismiss, ignore, or regulate to lower status. Conservation is what governs us now—at the local, national, and international level—and should always be the first issue on the table in the boardrooms when decisions are made.

We talk now of this episode as a sort of "Prague Spring" for our personal faith in those local people like us who hope to save the valley of Lawson's Fork. Instead of tanks it was bulldozers and skidders that rolled through the forests of our valley.

I know that what we've created in our minds out here is an imagined frontier, what Paige West says anthropologists call "the beyond." The land along Lawson's Fork has become for us the place, as Paige says, where our "images, ideas, and dreams" can take hold, but what happens here, she suggests, is also always what destroys them: people can spend their whole lives looking for it, and "will never find what they are looking for."

> Driving is a spectacular form of amnesia. Everything is
> to be discovered, everything to be obliterated.
>
>   JEAN BAUDRILLARD, *America*

Driving the Circle with Fred

The first day of summer, June 21, Fred Parrish and I set out
from my house to drive the circle. It's 9 a.m. and still cool when
he picks me up in his Jeep Cherokee, but the weather calls for
a red-hot South Carolina high of ninety-five by midday. We're
out to drive the whole thing, to really circle—no more out and
back exploring of one area or another. This is it—we're finally
putting what Terry would call some full ground-truthing into
this narrative, some hard labor in time and space.

The old topo is folded on my lap. Looking down, the first
thing I notice is that our route is really no race course. There
isn't a single road that circles our house a mile out in all directions. There are only three or four segments of the perimeter line I've drawn where we can actually drive. We start west
and then quickly turn back almost due north. We leave Tempo
Court, turn left on Mustang Drive, a right on Starline Drive,
across Fairlane Drive, another right and we're on Lake Forest
Drive, leaving the Ford products behind.

I sense the boundary of the circle's edge arching ahead of me like the Berlin Wall or the Iron Curtain, but I know it's all in my head. There's no real boundary out there one mile from my house. It's only a circle I drew on a map with a saucer, a literary trick I've played on myself for three years to help write this story.

"The circle is abuilding," Fred says as he accelerates through an alley of ranch houses approaching fifty years old. I tell him that by the time we get home at noon the circle will be "abuilt," that this is the last, or next to last, chapter. If we were going to travel the whole circle we'd have to walk. Instead we'll zig and zag in Fred's Jeep from point to point on paved roads.

I've carried this map around now for years, and it's marked up and frayed on the seams from folding and refolding. I look down at it, and I ponder Pierce Acres intently, or at least I ponder its symbolic equivalent. The subdivision I've driven through once or twice daily shows up only as a patch of green filling the north of the circle, thick with a pattern of little black dots lining the streets. The map's not much help in real space like this. What do these little black dots representing houses really have to do with the ranch houses and the families inside we're passing? What does ink on a map have to do with their yards?

Besides that, this map was first drawn in 1927, compiled again from aerial photographs taken in 1976, field-checked in 1977, and then edited again in 1983. So what's on the topo is really what was here almost thirty years ago. I tell Fred, and he looks around, says that the next time they edit it they'll have to print it green for all the trees planted by new homeowners in the past thirty years.

After we turn onto Lake Forest there's a half-mile straight shot to the top of the ridge where we will actually slide along the circle for a while. Lake Forest Drive connects Woodburn Road with Fernwood-Glendale Road, and it's the central artery through the circle. The Lake Forest crossing of Lawson's Fork below us is one of only two auto bridges in the circle, and through most of the 1970s the other half of it down there was known as Snake Road because of its curves. "Tom Pierce sure saw something way out here. He developed this east end of Lake Forest first, all these woods, and he left the glory land of the dairy and west Lake Forest for much much later," Fred says, looking around at the old split-levels and ranches as we pass. "When Lake Forest finally opened up on that other end across the creek it was high glory for house building. Every sensible woman in town wanted to be there."

Headed up Lake Forest we're driving through the early 1960s, perfect as a movie set. There are blocks and blocks of these rectangular ranch houses and lots mimicking the early 1960s suburbs in every city in America. Most of the houses are ranch style, but each offers a slightly different façade, set the same distance back from the street on large acre lots. It's like the dream of a particular cultural moment caught in amber.

When we built our house we tried hard to avoid the particular period of landscaping memorialized here—the 1960s green sward of uniformly cut grass with what landscapers call "a green moustache" of shrubbery on each side of the front door. But nothing's that simple. After almost fifty years, the lots along Lake Forest are now a mixture of full lawns and a more recent development we embraced fully—breaking up lawns with irregularly shaped areas either natural or mulched. We drive past plantings in these islands of river birch, dogwood, Japanese maples, and crape myrtle interspersed with the region's native hardwoods—red oak, white oak, sweet gum, and tulip poplar.

Mulch is now as large a part of a landscaper's equation as grass once was. I note how many of the trees in the neighborhood are dressed with "volcano mulching," the recent popular practice of putting cones of dark mulch around the trunks. To a sociologist, "volcano mulching" dates these lots just as clearly as unbroken lawns once would have—early 1990s industrial park influence?

But the houses are aging well. I tell Fred I still get a strange comfort when I drive home down this street. My dream when I was a kid was to live in one of these brick houses in the suburbs. This was as good as it got for a poor boy used to the crumbling mill houses and neighborhoods on the north side of town.

There was a great deal to praise about the suburbs. These houses on Lake Forest were "backyard connected," one long-time resident of the neighborhood told me. He said Pierce Acres felt like an island neighborhood in the middle of no-where. If he really wanted to take "the scenic route" he'd head down Snake Road into town across the creek and through the dairy. Some of the streets weren't paved until the mid-1960s, and they played neighborhood touch football games on the side streets and in the empty lots.

He also liked the diversity they sensed here back then. It wasn't diversity as we define it today, but even though there were mostly ranch-style houses, they didn't all look exactly alike, and the people were moving into Spartanburg from everywhere. My contact had moved here with his family from Virginia, and his neighbors in Pierce Acres were from Michigan, Massachusetts, and England.

"One guy across the street moved in, and the first thing he did was cut down all his trees," he said. "They couldn't figure out what was going on. Most people planted trees in their yards. 'I grew up in Kansas,' the new neighbor said when asked, by way of explanation. 'We didn't have trees in our neighborhood there.' "

Fred thinks naturally about things like ridges, valleys, and the creeks at the bottom of them, and he has since he was a kid. He grew up on Woodburn Road in a big two-story rambling brick house on the ridge that's two miles south behind us. He moved there in the early 1950s when he was about ten, after his mother's brief early marriage over in Greenville had ended in divorce.

Fred's father was Dillwyn Parrish, the oldest son of painter Maxfield, some say the most popular American artist until Norman Rockwell succeeded him in the 1940s. Fred only saw his famous grandfather once, but he did know his grandmother, Lydia Parrish, who wrote *Slave Songs of the Georgia Sea Islands*. She lived mostly on St. Simons Island off the Georgia coast. Fred says he was supposed to spend the summer of 1953 with her in New Hampshire, at The Oaks, Maxfield Parrish's house in Cornish, but his grandmother died in March of that year.

When the marriage to Dillwyn broke up, his mother moved Fred and his brother to Spartanburg and married again to Tom Dashiell, a good man with an executive job in the textile business. They'd lived in Converse Heights at first, then built further out at the end of Woodburn Road where the textile executives and their families were living on the ridge.

On the land below where Fred grew up stretched several hundred acres of the old Springdale Dairy, owned by textile magnate Victor Montgomery. The Lawson's Fork creek bottoms below that were where the dairy grew corn for silage to feed the herd of champion milk cows. I was looking forward to later in the morning when the circle would carry us back through that area and deeper into Fred's thicket of memories.

*At the end of Lake Forest Drive we turn right on Fernwood-*Glendale Road, and we're finally riding the outer curve of the circle, exactly one mile from our house. I see we're already tending south, on the road down to Glendale. Fred's poking along, and cars pile up behind us. He's not noticing. You can tell he's driving to another drummer, one playing a tune composed fifty years in the past.

"Turn here," I say, trying to keep us as close to the circle's perimeter as I can and also listen to where Fred wants to take me at the same time. We head further south down Pineview Road. Fred's finally excited about the present because we're in such mixed country here. There are cow pastures on our right and little brick sixties ranches on our left, and the subdivision known as Calhoun Lakes stretches along the border of the pastures. This is the land Middleton Bagwell settled in the eighteenth century. Somewhere out there is the old family cemetery, but I haven't been able to get anyone to take me there yet. It sits somewhere on this ridge, a twin to the one where William Bagwell is buried on the other side of the creek, and I'd like to see it sometime. Last year an old high school friend brought me over here and told me he could take me right to the cemetery, that he'd played around in it as a child growing up in Calhoun Lakes, but when we got on the ground he lost his way and blamed it on all the new construction obliterating his childhood landmarks.

Soon Fred and I pass a little frame house we both admire in the middle of a big fenced yard with old fashioned hollyhocks growing in sprawling flowerbeds. The man who lives here has built a scale model of a pioneer village with log cabins in the side yard, and there's a ten-foot green plastic Statue of Liberty with a working red street light in her torch among his tomato plants out back. Fred's seen him in the yard and says, "He looks like somebody highly skilled as a machinist, you know, a fix-it kind of fellow."

I've driven friends out to Pineview Drive many times to gawk at the green plastic Statue of Liberty and yard ornaments surrounding it, but this morning Fred helps me see it with his eyes. There's creativity to what this man has done with his acre of my circle. Fred worked most of his life at a textile mill with men like this—"fix-it guys" as he calls them—not professors like I've worked with, so I know he has more tolerance for these "outsider art" diversions. What I've made fun of with my out-of-town friends, Fred infuses with a sort of wacky dignity. "Lord have mercy, look at his gardenias," Fred says, slowing down even more as we pass the little house with the yard ornaments. He rolls the window down to smell the blossoms from the road.

At the end of Pineview Drive we turn left onto Pecan Drive, a little paved piece of the Old Georgia Road. It's the same trail I've explored passing Manning's house on the other side of the creek. I tell Fred about it and how it was one of the primary roads for piedmont settlers.

"I'm stripping away all this asphalt and pine," Fred says, slowing down even more. "I'm seeing those iron wheels going through the dust." We pass a huge white oak. "Two hundred and fifty or three hundred years old, I don't know," Fred speculates looking up into the limbs of the oak. "One thing's sure, that tree saw the wagons pass."

Leaving Pecan Drive behind we head southeast to where the perimeter of the circle includes the old mill village of Glendale. Soon we pass the Glendale Methodist church. Fred slows down. It's abandoned, vacant, or decommissioned, whatever it is they do with churches once the congregation gets too small to support them. The historic wood frame structure dates back nearly to the nineteenth century, and the cemetery beside it may go back even further.

What Fred notices as we pull past the church is that the yard is an accident of natural history, that the space has been taken over by an innocent looking yellow flower in the last year or so: "Spotted Cat's Ear, an aggressive invasive that will soon be everywhere." I notice that several people sitting on porches are watching us drive by like we're the aggressive invasive on this day.

And why not? Most who drive through Glendale see it now for what it could be—a quaint gentrified village if Spartanburg ever grows this way again—rather than what it is, a final refuge for the truly affordable housing in the county. Many recent residents moved here because the rents are cheap and the leases loose. If someone cruises through like we're doing, they're probably thinking about something that very little good can come of for the few old timers who've lived here since the mill closed in 1961.

On the back street I notice that the houses are quite beautiful though. Like the ranch-style houses in Pierce Acres they are another architectural snapshot of the past: small wooden 1920s bungalows with full porches and a few Craftsman design details like a front-gabled roof and exposed roof rafters.

"That would cost two hundred thousand dollars in some gentrified old mill village near Durham or Chapel Hill," I say as we pass one particularly sharply tended little bungalow and yard. But in Spartanburg County it's worth only thirty thousand dollars even though it's only a mile from the country club golf course.

"Even the curb stones have history," I say, and tell Fred the story of the WPA workers recycling the gneiss markers used as headstones for the dead Revolutionary War soldiers for curbs. Now the stones are still serving their civic duty, and the historic graves are forgotten in the woods upstream from the mill dam.

When we reach the bottom of the hill we turn left and pass the James Bivings house, built by the mill's founder in 1835. Abandoned for decades, the Greek revival mansion is often open to the weather. It's owned by someone who will neither fix it up nor sell it. The best effort he's made is to put a cyclone fence up around the property and hope that kids don't burn it down like they did the old mill.

Just past the Bivings house we catch a glimpse of the creek falling over Glendale Shoals. "I love to look out and see through there to the run," Fred says. "I love water over rock."

*The stretch of road across Lawson's Fork has been straight-*ened, so drivers get up quite a head of steam when they roar

down the hill. We wait for everyone to pass through before finally turning back onto Clifton-Glendale Road. Leaving Glendale we cross the creek on the new concrete bridge, which was
constructed while I was in high school in the 1970s. Until then
all the traffic in and out of the village went down Broadway
and over the rusted steel-beamed bridge just upstream from
the dam.

I don't see that it's an improvement. Nobody notices the
creek anymore or the historic village nearby, but most of the
events that bring us down to Glendale happen on the old steel
structure—fund-raising parties for SPACE, picnics on cool fall
days. I even use the bridge for an outdoor classroom when I
take my Wofford students to the creek. The new bridge and
straightened county road is part of what Baudrillard meant
when he said that driving obliterates a landscape. The new
bridge and the road that approaches it destroy the larger community's sense of what Glendale is. Now it's simply a place to
be bypassed, a place apart from the flow of modern day-to-day
life.

Out of Glendale our route follows close on the course of a
road called Dogwood Circle and swings behind the old William
Bagwell farm. I tell Fred about the Bagwell cemetery and I find
it strange he doesn't remember if he's ever seen it, so we dip
through the back gates of Glenn Forest and revisit the quiet
spot I'd seen for the first time with Manning Lynch the year
before.

At first I have a little trouble finding the cemetery driveway,
but finally we slip through the side yard of one of a line of
houses on what the Glenn Forest developers called Old House
Road. For a moment I know from my old maps we're riding a
remnant of the Old Georgia Road again, this time on the other
side of the circle. For some reason I can be quite nostalgic about
a two-hundred-year-old road now lost under a subdivision.

It's early summer, and the poison ivy is already thick around the old Bagwell burying ground in a few patches where there's sun. I see that since I was here last, lightning has shattered the huge hemlock in the center of the cemetery and left the top sprawled outside the fence. Someone from the neighborhood's cut it into pieces and left it to rot beside the fence.

We pass through the big black gothic iron gate that says "Bagwell," and I see now that the standing trunk of the old hemlock, though decapitated, is still alive. A filigree of green branches hangs down on all sides. It's not very noble, but it's a survivor and I admire its stubborn nature. We walk over to the side hidden from our view, and Fred looks for the lightning scar, and there it is, a vertical crack down the tree's length. "Smote from above," Fred says, putting his hand deep in the crack.

Standing in front of the white marble line of Bagwell stones I commune for a moment with Gertrude. I think about what John Updike has said, how the Scots believed that in the end we should be "conscious of no more grass than will cover our own graves," and note that Gertrude has no grass at all. Her plot is covered with decaying leaves, a few rotting hemlock needles and branches, and a little gravel, but she's not a Scot either, with her English surname.

I wonder what she would think about this family cemetery fifteen years after she was probably the last Bagwell ever to enter eternal rest here, under this old piedmont tree and encircled at a peaceable distance by suburbia. It would probably disappoint her that the fancy black wrought iron fence she installed for protection has been vandalized, someone cutting half the ornate cast-iron finials off with a hacksaw. Would she now regret spending a chunk of her profit from selling the farm to install these white marble replacement stones? Would she be sad that the cemetery is now unknown to almost everyone, even those on the streets crisscrossing her old farm? Does she sleep soundly sequestered for eternity in this tract of hardwoods?

Gertrude doesn't answer, so I formulate a few judgments of

my own. The finials bother me most, probably lost one by one to some high school fraternity's teenage initiation rite, but then I remember my friend's story of the night duty demanded by the Glendale boys of the 1950s, how they had to steal a chip from an original Bagwell stone and bring it back the next morning to match it up. Maybe vandalizing the past is just the way one generation makes space for the next. After all, there's only so much space. They're not making any more of it, as they like to say.

But what space is sacred or should be? What space should be beyond Baudrillard's obliteration? Shouldn't a cemetery almost two hundred years old qualify for protection by more than the local law? Shouldn't everyone have bred within them some deep respect for such a place?

We walk outside the fence and wander just west of the enclosed ground and see that the woods around are thick with old stones, so even the Bagwells did their own editing of the space. They fenced off what they wanted to save, letting some of the dead in and keeping others out. Fred scratches one or two of the hidden stones and says, "Wow. These are old—made of soapstone."

I see the white line trailing along where his nail passed and know Fred's right—soapstone. The soft local stone was readily available to the pioneers from eight or nine sites in Spartanburg County, one of them less than five miles away. Settlers secured it from outcrops for cooking pots just like the Archaic period bands passing up the creek thousands of years ago. They also utilized its easy carving for burying stones in spots like the Bagwell cemetery.

We bend close to read what's left, but the writing has been worked down by time. We talk for a moment of recovering these stones from the weeds with mowers and bush hogs, but that will have to wait for another day.

After leaving the Bagwell cemetery we drop down the west

side of the circle through the drainage of Four Mile Branch. Out here it's not much of a creek to speak of. We're a mile or so from its confluence with Lawson's Fork, the spot where Buffington had set up his ironworks in 1760, but the creek's so small here you could jump across it. We follow the creek for a little ways anyway, and Fred says he seems to remember that the headwaters are up on the Highway 176 ridge coming out of a big petroleum tank farm at Camp Croft, and that back a few decades he says he thinks Four Mile Branch actually caught fire like that river up in Cleveland. "I can't remember exactly when it was, but I remember it happened," Fred says as we follow the creek on into the circle.

We continue through the valley of Four Mile Branch, and Fred likes what he sees back up in here: "What a mixed neighborhood. Look at that big old damn house and compare it to what's just down the street. You used to see the same type of integration down on the coast when some little plank house worth about a thousand dollars was next to someone who was Lord Have Mercy rich."

We hit Country Club Road then turn left onto Woodburn Road and approach the circle again from the south. I can sense the affluence hanging in the air. Fred's memory really gets cranked up as we make the turn onto Woodburn, but the 1950s he's remembering were simpler times: "Back then when I was growing up there was none of this flash and glitter that you see now. We had the Powell twins, and Hurkey Montgomery, who were sort of our local celebs. Hurkey's daddy was Victor, and they had Springdale Dairy. But otherwise most everybody I knew, their daddy had a quiet insurance job, or worked at the bank, or with one of the mills like my daddy."

As we ride on down Woodburn Road Fred continues to talk about the neighborhood as he remembers it: "Back in fifty-five you didn't have all these pine trees. Everything below us was a pasture for the dairy, and from this ridge you could see the mountains." He points out some more of his neighbors as we drive along. "The Cates lived up there and that's where the Powells lived. Their daddy had Powell Knitting Mill. Their mama was Caro Cleveland. They were redheaded and walked in a kind of mist, had the first Raleigh bicycles in the neighborhood. There was this mystery about them."

Fred could tell I was wandering off a little with all this genealogy of the Spartanburg blue bloods, and so he added: "The Powell twins are not important, but they are a distinct entity in the soil horizon labeled Spartanburg, 1945–1960, as if we were looking at one of Terry Ferguson's deposition layers from, say, the late Archaic period, down at the creek."

Though up here on the ridge top we're officially out of the circle, I don't really want to stop Fred's reminiscing. We're in that territory for part of the morning where my circle and Fred's overlap, and I've just got to hear him out and realize it's all connected. It's somebody's circles all the way out until we come around the other side of the globe.

I tell Fred I want to take my regular route home and drive down Lake Forest Drive, but Fred insists we go on down to Montgomery Drive and turn there because "there was no Lake Forest Drive back when I was growing up. There was only a farm road from the dairy up to our mama's land, just a lane that a tractor could use."

In Fred's childhood, Montgomery Drive was a magic land. Down at the end of it sat Greylogs, the weekend log cabin home for many years of textile magnate Victor Montgomery, namesake of the drive. The road was paved down to the gates of Greylogs, and then it turned to dirt and continued on south down into the creek bottom, crossed the creek, and then turned north to run past Pierce Lake.

Near the intersection of Woodburn and Montgomery Drives Fred gets excited and points out where in 1959 there was a red oak grove "way out in the cow pasture on the Cates' land."

Cates, with Montgomery, was one of the legendary early mill owners living on the ridge. Fred says a big red-tailed hawk sat there year after year. One of the big red oaks died, and Fred told Mac Sr. he'd cut it up for ten dollars. "That was in the days when people were making eighty-five cents a day at the mill."

Mac took him up on it. Fred worked on the tree for two weeks, "even got my buddies out there helping." When Fred finished he went to Mac Sr. "The old man's eyes danced a lot when he was onto something, and they were dancing when he asked, 'Boy, you learn anything out there cutting on that granddaddy oak?' Well, I learned about hard work. He was one granddaddy oak himself."

Now the old fields are filled with expensive houses on large lots softened by trees, the land sold off parcel by parcel in the 1960s and 1970s to fulfill the high-end suburban dreams of dozens of Spartanburg's wealthier east-siders. On Montgomery Drive live mill presidents, tycoons, doctors, dentists, even Frederick B. Dent, former Secretary of Commerce under Gerald Ford, a Yale graduate who came to Spartanburg in 1947 to work in textiles.

Just past the Dents' imposing yellow Colonial Revival on Montgomery there's a one-story white Craftsman-style house with black shutters that clearly doesn't fit this affluent neighborhood. It was probably built in the 1920s with clapboard siding and a nice porch and commands a spot right on top of the last knoll before the land slopes away to the creek bottom below. Fred sweeps his arms around and says the barns for the dairy were right over there to the right, and huge silos loomed somewhere nearby where Springdale Dairy kept silage to feed the cows. "If I could walk over there I could show you the foundations," he says.

We are in the middle of what used to be Springdale Dairy's operation, and Fred remembers it all: "I can tell you a whole lot about the dairy," he says. "They got sludge from the sewer plant and spread it all over that pasture. There were displaced people working here just like in the Flannery O'Connor short story. They came from Germany and Poland. They had a big silage operation. I can smell that sweet richness right now."

Fred comes to a complete stop in the Jeep Cherokee, sits in the road, and points down toward where the corn had been grown in the bottoms "so they didn't have to depend on the pastures so much. Those big bull thistles you see summers on Lake Forest Drive? They came here in a load of hay from Canada one year in the fifties when it was so dry there was no corn and no pasture grass."

He tells me how as a boy he'd roamed out over the dairy pastures: "On that hillside that butts up to the country club, where the sewer pipe now runs, they had the chain gang cutting brush one week with bank blades. We were going along the sewer pipe, thirteen years old. I spotted a striped jacket on that hillside, big wide black and white stripes. I was the first one to it. You just know some things. I took it home and got it washed and wore it from then on. One day I was over at George Dean and Stewart Johnson's mama's house. Betty Johnson took one look at me in that prisoner's jacket and said, 'Freddy, I don't understand how your mother can allow you to wear that horrid thing.' But there were four or five teenagers that would have killed for that jacket."

We begin to descend toward the floodplain and we pull into the driveway for Greylogs, the old cabin now secluded behind pines and azaleas. Fred wants to continue on down the driveway and show the house to me, but I stop him and say I don't want to drop in on the present owners, whom I don't know. Fred stops in the drive and talks about the pool, how "it was spring fed, even up into my childhood."

It's really tempting to go on down to the cabin. I've seen photos taken in 1925, and back then Victor Montgomery's place looked like something you'd see in the Adirondacks or Maine, a long, rustic one-story cabin with fieldstone foundations, a big deer head over the fireplace, and rough hewn logs for rafters.

Old Victor Montgomery, who built Greylogs, had been dead twenty years by the time Fred wandered the old dairy. Victor's son raised all three of his children at Greylogs, and then in the late fifties, a few years after Fred's family settled out here, he sold the dairy to the Pierces, who continued to run it until the midsixties. Pacolet Mills was sold to the Millikens, and Victor moved out of the textile business and into real estate, carving up what was left of the high ground for houses. Victor the Second died in 1970, and his son, the third Victor, was the one Fred had known as "Hurkey."

It must have been a time when it felt to Fred like giants were walking the land out here. "There have only been three owners since old Victor built it—Charlie Green, Henry Blackford, and now the Dulkens. Unchanged in fifty-five years," Fred says as he backs out of the Greylogs drive.

Near the end of Montgomery Drive we turn left next to a modern ranch-style split-level crossed with Tudor and follow a long road called Somerset that dead-ends near the creek. The houses along Somerset have to be perilously close to the limits of Lawson's Fork's one-hundred-year floodplain, but so far they have survived the rising waters. Some of the houses have pastures, and the landscape harkens back to the pastoral Springdale Dairy years. When we're turning around in one driveway we see that rather than livestock though, there's a flock of ten or twelve wild turkeys scratching comfortably in the side yard. They seem unconcerned that we've punctuated their grazing with our visit, and Fred says seeing the flock is a good sign for the creek valley. We both agree we'd rather see wild turkeys than cows in Lawson's Fork's future.

Crossing the creek on Lake Forest Drive we pull over and look down the narrow alley opened into the floodplain by the country club's clear-cut. It's been a year since our fight to save it, and we've had to drive past every day. There are now two bulldozers, a grader, and three dump trucks clearing debris and leveling the tract, probably for the driving range the club's always hoped to have. "People react to a clear-cut in this region the way they react to blood from a scalp wound," Walter Kaufman says in *Coming out of the Woods*. "Usually, however, the face covered with blood does not signal a broken skull or severed brains; but clear-cutting clouds the brains of reasonable people."

The insult to the place has grown stronger if anything. "This clear-cut really shook Betsy and me up," I say. "We still haven't recovered. It shook us deep."

What is it exactly? Fred asks, and I try to explain. We were so new to this landscape and we wanted to suspend it in our own drop of amber. Places just don't suspend very well in amber. "They're just too valuable for one reason or another," I say, looking across seventy acres of cleared ground.

Fred's seen this circle go from agriculture to raw real estate and field, into suburbs in fifty years as "town" has crept closer and closer to "country" because of sprawl, better roads, and the dreams of hundreds of people. All we've seen since we arrived is this little bit of botched development.

"Look at that rich earth," Fred says, marveling at the dark, deep topsoil of the bottomland hidden all of fifty years by the country club's crop of now-harvested hardwoods. Fred sees in his memory the open bottomland of his childhood growing silage for the Springdale dairy herd. I still see that wild piedmont forest there when we moved in and its promise of wildlife, secluded hiking. It was our little savings account against all the past and present development around us in the circle. But it wasn't our account, and the arguments we made to "save" it made little sense to those who controlled the property.

We make one more side trip after we leave the clear-cut. We drive up Torino Drive so Fred can see the most expensive house in the circle now under construction—a three-story stone and slate castle costing maybe as much as four million dollars going up on what's always been known as Pierce Lake. "It looks like Biltmore House up in Asheville," Fred says, laughing, as we park for a moment in front of the showy mansion on the lake. I joke about how Victor Montgomery was happy living out here in a log cabin, and he was probably a great deal richer than these folks.

Fred reminds me that Victor also had his mansion in town though. Things are never as simple as I'd like them to be.

As if it were a scene made up by the mind,
That is not mine, but is a made place.

ROBERT DUNCAN, "Often I am Permitted
to Return to a Meadow"

EPILOGUE

Is

The circle tightens as Fred and I drive the final three blocks to
our house on Tempo Court. What have I gained from circling
out and back through this tiny scrap of southern landscape? I
have found some assurance that I've finally settled, but the ba-
sic trappings of settlement—marriage, family, home—are not
enough. Even Elijah Clarke, our first pioneer, would have understood those terms. A few years after building his cabin on
the Pacolet, Clarke moved on to the wilder frontier. Already by
1775 the woods and river bottoms I love were not wild enough
for him. He traveled down the Old Georgia Road into what was
still Indian country.

I want some deeper understanding of what's at stake now
in the valley of Lawson's Fork. There are no frontiers Clarke
would recognize out my backdoor. I have traded the freedom of
frontiers for what Frank Lloyd Wright calls "organic simplicity,"
the integration of the necessary functions of a modern human
life with natural beauty.

Betsy and I have tried to find that simplicity. We've worked to make our house part of a larger whole reflected in the woods and water around us. Using Wright as a mentor, we built our unusual house to mimic the colors and arrangements we saw in this piedmont landscape. We embraced what Wright called "freedom of floor space" through our open floor plan. We try to live lightly, reducing what's now known as a "carbon footprint" by a dozen choices for better energy use. Often we're reminded of it by something as simple as light through the south-facing windows or rain falling on our tin roof. "Living within a house wherein everything is genuine and harmonious," Wright wrote, "a new sense of freedom gives one a new sense of life."

When Fred turns onto Tempo Court I can see the result of all our reflection and planning. Our house is hard to see at the end of the cul-de-sac. With its granite gray wall, tan hues, and reflecting glass it blends into the summer woods that close in around it. Only the driveway and the mailbox announce that someone's home is deep in the trees.

Fred pulls in the driveway and remembers before he leaves that he's promised he'll fix my brush mower. The belt slips when I'm cutting in heavy grass, and our paths down to the creek are overgrown. He asks me if I've got a pair of "channel-lock pliers," and we both marvel at the names of things, some-times perfect little poems that grab you and hold on like the pliers themselves. He knows exactly what to do with the pliers: unloosens four bolts, pulls the belt back into place, tightens them back down, and it's ready to go. A real fix-it guy.

Fred says he's got a lunch appointment with his daughter and says goodbye. After he leaves, I crank up the big roaring mower and head it down the hill. I cut the edges of the path leading out of our backyard down to the creek. Once down on the trail I cut a four-foot swath thirty yards in either direction. With that finished, I head the machine back up the hill. I'll do the rest later.

The irony of my big gas-burning trail mower isn't lost on me. I think of our trails as sort of "linear lawns" and know I probably spend as much time mowing them as my neighbors do their yards. My taste is trails and theirs lawns. A long mile along the road to settlement is making peace with other people's taste.

I need to keep the trails cut because the creek is really why we are out here on the edge of the suburbs. The real bull's-eye of my circle is not the house. It's down where the water flows. That eternal flow is what sustains my attention through drought and flood. They used to believe that all rivers flowed from the center of the earth, but now we know that's not true. Rivers are simply a part of the great cycle of water circulation on the planet, the great pattern of evaporation from earth to atmosphere and back again, over and over.

The dogs have their patterns too. When I go inside they are frantic to get out, so we walk the newly mowed trail down to the creek for a minute so that they can get out of the house after a long morning on the couch. The heat's rising and we won't be out long, though it's quickly cooler under the trees down next to the water.

I listen for a moment to the creek falling over a log or two lodged in current and sand. When we reach the high bank, it seems something unseen by me has passed earlier, and Toby's almost crazy with the trail. Within a week of moving in, Betsy saw a bobcat on this very river-bottom trail. Deer wander into the yard every evening. A red-shouldered hawk hunts from a dead snag along the shore. Rob saw a family of raccoons getting acquainted with our garbage can late one night after they waddled up the trail at dusk. During a thunderstorm I watched a possum lope slowly through newly sprouted wildflowers on the backyard's sloping expanse, headed for the sanctuary of the creek bottom.

Toby pulls against the leash, but I know he'll disappear into the bottom if I let him, and we might not see him for days.

What freedom he senses right off the end of my short leash. Once again I consider just cutting my aging couch hound loose and letting him run like the bottom dog he longs to be. He's ten years old now. If he comes back, all the better. If he doesn't, he'll have disappeared a happy beagle. I just can't do it though. He owes me too much companionship yet to let him go.

There are human leashes, and settling is one. It's been such a good morning, so full of delight and surprise, I can't imagine complicating it with such an idea. Ellie heads up the path. I tug Toby back toward home.

As we're walking, I remember how when Toby's ready to go out he always turns in a tight circle at my feet until I snap on the leash and head out the door. I end this trip with some circling of my own right here at the center of my universe. I drop Toby's leash, and they watch me as I spin. I see the trees and sky turning above me, watch the creek and our house flashing past with equal intensity. If I spin hard enough, I just might screw myself so deep into this spot I'd be planted here forever, or at least as close to forever as is humanly possible.

Acknowledgments

Environmental historians and the ecocritics often talk about the "layered history" of a particular place. Recently, GIS technology has taken this idea even further, producing actual layered models of space and time in which you can add or subtract any information set you choose—topography, population, geology, plant life, industry, school districts, voting records, and so forth.

A traditional narrative still offers a similar perspective, and it's important to document where the data arrived from during the long process of composition. Saying thanks to friends, contacts, and sources is a writer's way of plotting points on a sort of relational graph of a community.

What follows is a list of local people who helped me discover the mile around our house, followed by a short but by no way exhaustive list of the books and documents I kept close at hand as I composed this story.

I'll start with the people I talked with before and during the writing of this story. I ask that all realize how much local "history" has to give way to the demands of story once a project like this gets underway. I tried to be as accurate as possible with all you shared, but I do not pretend that this is not, first and foremost, a personal narrative. I suggest to anyone who does not like the world that I see around me that you draw your own circle on a map and write your own book.

Wofford College sociology professor and writer Gerald Thurmond read this manuscript in the final stages of composition and made dozens of comments that both improved and deepened this story. Friend and dean of southern environmental historians, Jack Temple Kirby, also read several of the chapters in draft and offered suggestions to sharpen the content. Wofford College geologist and archeologist Terry Ferguson agreed once again to show up as a character in one of my narratives, and he was instrumental in helping me understand the landscape around me. Terry is a tireless observer of the world, and without him I could never have shaped these experiences into a story. South Carolina Institute of Archeology staff member Tommy Charles and Wofford College biology professor Doug Rayner both walked the land with me. Savannah River Ecology Lab researcher and native of the circle David Scott played golf and answered my e-mails.

I can't thank Fred Parrish enough for all he contributed through e-mails, conversation, and companionship. This is as much his circle as it is mine.

I'd also like to thank Susan Thoms in the Kennedy Room at the headquarters of the Spartanburg County Public Library and Carolyn Creal, formerly at the Regional Museum of Spartanburg County. Both are fine local historians, and they were always helpful and thorough when I showed up in their archives, often looking for old newspaper clippings and documents to fill out a scene. Many thanks also to Erin Knight at Upstate Forever for helping me see "the circle" more clearly by producing a great series of GIS maps of the territory.

For other support, conversation, and bits of insight I would like to thank the late Tommy Pierce, Kristy Pierce Drummer, Trey Pierce, Peyton and Alice Howell, Sebastian Matthews, B. G. Stephens, Richard Rankin, Janisse Ray, Dorinda Dallmeyer, David Beacham, Joe Lesesne, Lee Altman, Jim Seegars, Christine Swager, Doug Nash, Winston Haynes McElveen, Joe Hudson, Bill and Kristin Taylor, Steve and Penni Patton, Allyn

Steele, Martin Meek, Manning and Mary Speed Lynch, Paul and Sara Lehner, Don Wildman, Frank and Wendell Tiller. Foster Chapman, Randy Judy, and Norman Chapman were kind enough to allow me access to one of their private Saturday morning golf rounds. Many thanks to these three for the privilege of tagging along one day.

For reading the book when it was finished and doing a very important copyedit I will always be grateful to Lauren Stephenson. For technical support a special thanks goes as always to Wofford College's Cathy Conner who went beyond the call of duty to keep all my dozens of drafts straight and printed out on her magic machines.

A few human histories proved very helpful for context as I circled in my home state of South Carolina: David Ramsay's *History of South Carolina* (1808), John Logan's *History of Upper South Carolina* (1859), and J. B. O. Landrum's *Colonial and Revolutionary History of Upper South Carolina* (1897). Phil Racine's *Piedmont Farmer: the Journals of David Golightly Harris* (1990) helped me understand Harris's nineteenth-century "neighbors" the Bagwells. Michael Hembree and Paul Crocker's *Glendale: A Pictorial History* (1994) added to my understanding of that community. Walter Edgar's more recent *South Carolina: A History* (1998) also helped me, especially to understand the context of the American Revolution in this area.

A few more literary books were always close at hand throughout the process: *Go Down, Moses* (1942) by William Faulkner, *Spirit of Place: The Making of an American Literary Landscape* (1990) by Frederick Turner, and *Wild Fruits: Thoreau's Rediscovered Last Manuscript* (2000) by Henry David Thoreau.

For natural history questions, the texts I kept nearby were *To See a World* (1973) by geologist and mentor John Harrington; *A Naturalist's Guide to the Piedmont* by Michael A. Godfrey (1980); Luna Leopold's two classics of hydrology, *A View of the River* (1994) and *Water, Rivers and Creeks* (1997); *Reading the Forested Landscape* (1997) by Tom Wessels; *Time Before History* by

H. Trawick Ward and R. P. Stephen Davis (1999); and *A Guide to the Wildflowers of South Carolina* by Richard Dwight Porcher and Douglas Alan Rayner (2001).

Finally, I'd also like to acknowledge my debt to a few books of similar theme (exploring a landscape limited in some key factor like space or time) that inspired me throughout this project: *Ceremonial Time* (1984) by John Hanson Mitchell, *Seven Half-Miles from Home* (1985) by Mary Back, *PrairyErth* (1991) by William Least Heat-Moon, and *The Bones of the Earth* (2004) by Howard Mansfield.

For the time to read all these books I would like to thank the Interim Committee at Wofford College for an important month off one January a few years ago. I had no idea at the time the leave would cost me so much more work down the line, but I am grateful it did. Much gratitude is also due to Wofford president Bernie Dunlap, dean Dan Maultsby, and English Department chair Vivian Fisher for their continued professional encouragement of my parallel careers as professor and writer of personal narratives.

At the University of Georgia Press I would like to thank Judy Purdy, John McLeod, and Jon Davies, as well as freelance copyeditor Sue Breckenridge. UGA Press has shown important support for my work, and I will always be grateful.

My wife, Betsy Teter, as always has supported me every step of the way in my writing life and generously agreed to let me make her a main character in this story.

Finally, thanks also to my fine stepsons, Rob and Russell Teter, who both will appreciate their central roles in this story even more when they get some distance on them. Because of our efforts to build here I know there will always be a creek they love and a deep and wild floodplain below their "home place" in Spartanburg. That, in many ways, is the point of my telling this story.